I dedicate this book with love to
Craig Yoe,
an unending source of marvels.
Con amore a **Giovanna Anzaldi,** tuttologa,
e a **Nerio Gussoni,** esperto di molte cose.
–Clizia Gussoni

To my **family** with **love.**
–Luke McDonnell

The Awesome Book of SHARKS!

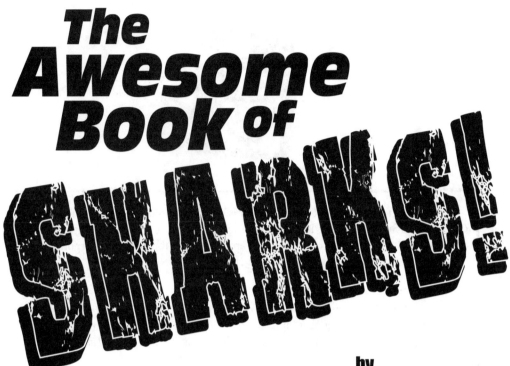

by
Clizia Gussoni

Illustrated by
Luke McDonnell

RUNNING PRESS
KIDS
PHILADELPHIA·LONDON

Italian born and trained, Clizia Gussoni is co-founder and Creative Director of Gussoni-Yoe Studio, Inc., a cutting-edge design firm housed in a mountaintop castle overlooking the Hudson River. Her clients are among the top names in corporate America: Disney, Warner Bros., Cartoon Network, MTV, Nickelodeon, Mattel, and Microsoft, to name but a few.

Clizia specializes in innovative design and creations and has garnered several awards in recognition of her accomplishments, including a Mobius and two Addys. She has been featured in various publications including *The New York Times, Li©ense! Magazine,* and *The Women's Business Journal.*

9   8   7   6   5   4   3   2
Digit on the right indicates the number of this printing

Library of Congress Control Number: 2006921854

ISBN-13: 978-0-7624-2644-7
ISBN-10: 0-7624-2644-6

This book may be ordered by mail from the publisher.
Please include $2.50 for postage and handling.
But try your bookstore first!

Published by Running Press Kids, an imprint of
Running Press Book Publishers
125 South Twenty-second Street
Philadelphia, Pennsylvania 19103-4399

Visit us on the web!
www.runningpress.com

Big, splashy **THANK YOUs** to the following people who, with their **creativity, patience,** and **dedication,** have made this book possible: Jon Anderson, Craig Yoe, the great illustrator Luke McDonnell, Jayne Antipow, Joy Court, Michael Tomolonis, Teresa Bonaddio, Mike Hill, Susan Shanti Gibian, Linda Salsedo, Chiara De Marchis, and Mom and Dad.
    —*Clizia Gussoni*

Thanks to all the **sharks** who posed for these pictures!
    —*Luke McDonnell*

Sharks are fascinating to me. They live in a treacherous and unfamiliar place, the ocean. We know very little about this environment; we feel like fish out of water there!

Sharks are mysterious fish. There's much more to sharks than the eating-machines Hollywood portrays them to be. They are older than dinosaurs and have sophisticated ways of communicating with each other. Sharks have sharp senses and are able to know where you are, even if they can't see you, perceiving the electric field you emanate.

Writing this book reminded me that we humans are not the only wonderful creatures on earth. We are surrounded by many others, and we should strive to live with full respect for all living things. Because the greatest predator of all, even greater than the mighty great white shark, is the human species.

Olizia.

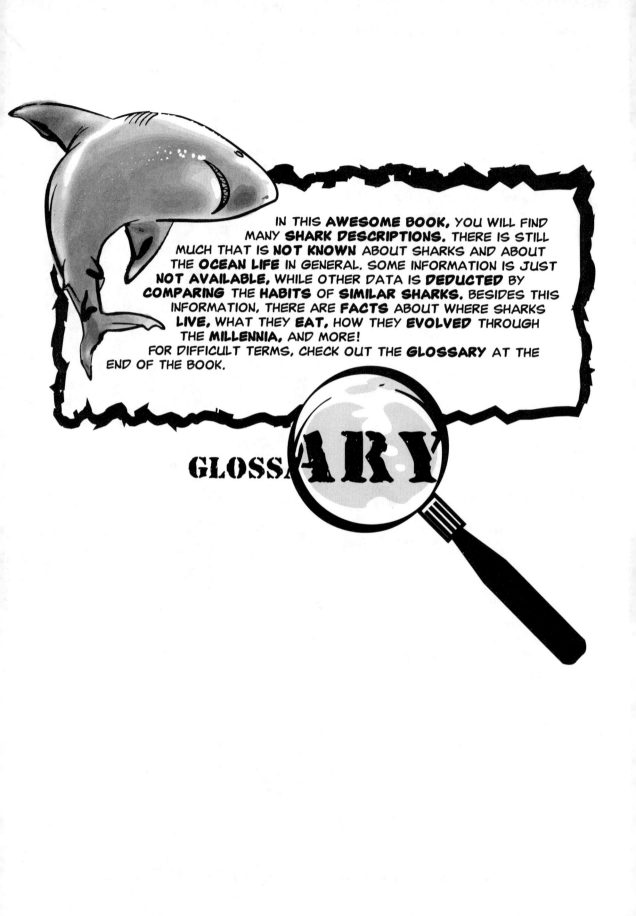

IN THIS **AWESOME BOOK,** YOU WILL FIND
MANY **SHARK DESCRIPTIONS.** THERE IS STILL
MUCH THAT IS **NOT KNOWN** ABOUT SHARKS AND ABOUT
THE **OCEAN LIFE** IN GENERAL. SOME INFORMATION IS JUST
NOT AVAILABLE, WHILE OTHER DATA IS **DEDUCTED** BY
COMPARING THE **HABITS** OF **SIMILAR SHARKS.** BESIDES THIS
INFORMATION, THERE ARE **FACTS** ABOUT WHERE SHARKS
LIVE, WHAT THEY **EAT,** HOW THEY **EVOLVED** THROUGH
THE **MILLENNIA,** AND MORE!
FOR DIFFICULT TERMS, CHECK OUT THE **GLOSSARY** AT THE
END OF THE BOOK.

GLOSSARY

WHAT IS A SHARK?

A scalloped hammerhead shark.

SHARKS ARE **CARNIVOROUS** AND **PREDATORY** FISH. THEY BELONG TO THE GROUP CALLED **CHONDRICHTHYES**, WHICH ARE FISH WITH A **SKELETON** MADE OF **CARTILAGE**. MOST OTHER FISH HAVE A **SKELETON** MADE OF **BONES**, AND ARE CALLED **OSTEICHTHYES**. THERE ARE ABOUT **400** DIFFERENT KINDS OF **SHARKS** IN THE WORLD!

BESIDES SHARKS, CHONDRICHTHYES ALSO INCLUDE **SKATES** AND **RAYS**.

A manta ray.

A skate.

SHARKS HAVE **FIVE TO SEVEN GILL SLITS** ON BOTH SIDES OF THEIR HEAD. **BONY FISH** HAVE THEIR **GILLS** COVERED WITH **FLAPS.**

BONY FISH RELY ON THEIR **AIR BLADDER** FOR **BALANCE** AND **BUOYANCY** IN THE WATER. SHARKS USE THEIR **LARGE, OIL-FILLED LIVER.**

A shark's liver.

Shark Tales: In the 18th century cabinetmakers used shagreen to polish wood. Shagreen was made from the skin of certain sharks and rays.

SHARK'S SKIN IS COVERED WITH LITTLE, HARD **SCALES,** EACH BEARING A VERY SMALL, TOOTH-LIKE **SPINE** POINTING BACKWARD.

A SHARK'S **SKELETON** IS MADE OF **CARTILAGE,** NOT OF BONE.

SHARK DETAILS

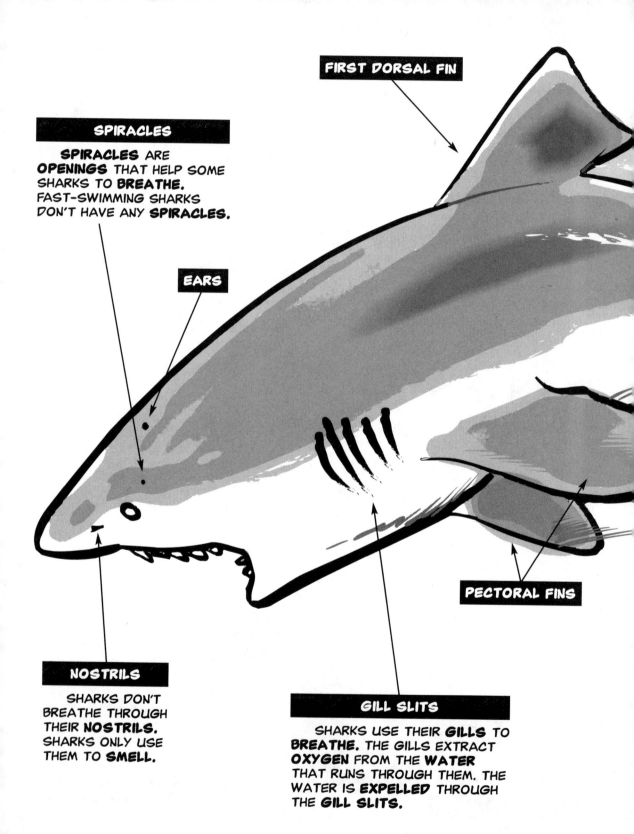

FIRST DORSAL FIN

SPIRACLES

SPIRACLES ARE **OPENINGS** THAT HELP SOME SHARKS TO **BREATHE.** FAST-SWIMMING SHARKS DON'T HAVE ANY **SPIRACLES.**

EARS

PECTORAL FINS

NOSTRILS

SHARKS DON'T BREATHE THROUGH THEIR **NOSTRILS.** SHARKS ONLY USE THEM TO **SMELL.**

GILL SLITS

SHARKS USE THEIR **GILLS** TO **BREATHE.** THE GILLS EXTRACT **OXYGEN** FROM THE **WATER** THAT RUNS THROUGH THEM. THE WATER IS **EXPELLED** THROUGH THE **GILL SLITS.**

A SHARK'S TAIL FIN HAS **TWO LOBES.** THE **TOP** IS GENERALLY **BIGGER** THAN THE **BOTTOM** ONE. THIS KIND OF TAIL IS CALLED **HETEROCERCAL,** FROM THE GREEK WORDS **HETEROS** ("DIFFERENT") AND **KERKOS** ("TAIL").

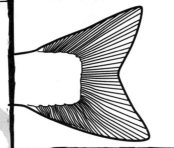

THE **TAIL LOBES** OF MOST **BONY FISH** ARE **SYMMETRICAL.** THIS KIND OF TAIL IS CALLED **HOMOCERCAL,** FROM THE GREEK WORDS **HOMO** ("SAME") AND **KERKOS** ("TAIL").

SECOND DORSAL FIN

PELVIC FINS

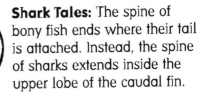

Shark Tales: The spine of bony fish ends where their tail is attached. Instead, the spine of sharks extends inside the upper lobe of the caudal fin.

ANAL FINS

CLASPER

ONLY **MALE SHARKS** HAVE CLASPERS.

CAUDAL FIN

THE CAUDAL FIN, OR **TAIL FIN,** IS MADE UP OF AN **UPPER** AND A **LOWER LOBE.**

SHARKS CAN **SEE** WELL, ESPECIALLY IN **DARK** AND **DEEP WATERS.** JUST LIKE IN HUMANS, SHARKS' **IRISES** CONTROL THE **PUPILS.** PUPILS CAN BECOME **WIDER** OR **NARROWER** TO REGULATE THE **AMOUNT** OF **LIGHT** THAT PENETRATES THE **EYE. BUT SHARKS' PUPILS** ARE **MORE EFFICIENT** THAN OURS AND CAN SEE **TEN TIMES BETTER.**

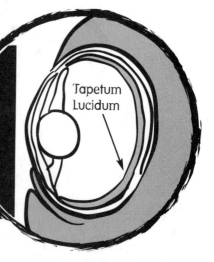

SHARKS' EYES HAVE A **LAYER** BEHIND THE **RETINA** CALLED **TAPETUM LUCIDUM.** THIS TERM COMES FROM THE LATIN AND MEANS **"BRIGHT CARPET."** THE TAPETUM LUCIDUM **REFLECTS** THE **LIGHT** BACK INTO THE EYE, SO THAT SHARKS CAN SEE **BETTER** THAN HUMANS IN **DIM LIGHT.** MANY **NOCTURNAL ANIMALS,** LIKE CATS, USE THIS SAME SYSTEM TO TAKE THE **BEST ADVANTAGE** OF THE **LITTLE LIGHT** PRESENT AT **NIGHT.**

Tapetum Lucidum

SHARKS HAVE SPECIAL **CELLS** IN THEIR EYES THAT ARE ABLE TO **DETECT COLORS.** THESE CELLS ARE CALLED **CONES,** AND HUMANS HAVE THEM TOO.

SOME SHARKS HAVE **NICTITATING MEMBRANES.** THESE ARE SPECIAL **EYELIDS** THAT **COVER** THE **EYES** OF THE SHARK WHEN THEY COULD GET **HARMED,** SUCH AS WHEN THE SHARK IS **STRUGGLING** WITH ITS **PREY.** UNLIKE OUR EYELIDS, SHARKS' **NICTITATING MEMBRANES** MOVE FROM THE **BOTTOM** OF THE EYES TO THE **TOP.** THE MEMBRANES ARE **WHITE** AND NOT ALL SHARKS HAVE THEM. THOSE WITHOUT THEM ARE ABLE TO **ROLL** THEIR **EYES** ALL THE WAY BACK INTO THEIR **EYE SOCKETS.**

NICTITATING MEMBRANE

SHARKS HAVE **TWO NOSTRILS** LOCATED ABOVE THEIR **SNOUT.** THEIR NOSTRILS ARE USED FOR **SMELLING,** BUT NOT FOR **BREATHING.**

NOSTRILS AREN'T CONNECTED TO A SHARK'S **LUNGS,** ONLY TO ITS **BRAIN.** SHARKS, LIKE ALL FISH, **BREATHE** WITH THEIR **GILLS.** THE SHARK'S **SENSE** OF **SMELL** IS SO **KEEN** IT CAN DETECT ONE **DROP** OF **BLOOD** IN ABOUT **30 GALLONS** OF **WATER.**

NOSTRILS

EACH NOSTRIL HAS **TWO OPENINGS.** THE **WATER** PASSES THROUGH THE NOSTRILS OVER THE SHARK'S **OLFACTORY LAMELLAE.** THESE **MEMBRANES** ARE ABLE TO **CAPTURE INFORMATION** ABOUT **SMELLS** AND **SEND SIGNALS** TO THE **BRAIN.** A SHARK'S SENSE OF SMELL IS VERY KEEN BECAUSE A **LARGE PART** OF ITS **BRAIN** IS DESIGNATED TO INTERPRET **SMELL INFORMATION.**

Source of scent.

WHEN SHARKS PICK UP THE **SCENT** OF THEIR PREY, THEY **COMPARE INFORMATION** DETECTED BY **ONE** OF THEIR **NOSTRILS** AND THEN THE **OTHER.** SHARKS **ADJUST** THEIR **PATH** UNTIL THEY REACH THEIR **PREY.**

ELECTRORECEPTION IS PROBABLY THE MOST **INTRIGUING** OF THE **SHARK'S SENSES.** EVERY **LIVING CREATURE** EMANATES AN **ELECTRIC FIELD** AND SHARKS ARE ABLE TO **DETECT** THE **INTENSITY** AND **DIRECTION** OF IT. SOME SHARKS CAN **LOCATE** AND **ATTACK** A PREY THAT IS HIDING **MOTIONLESS** UNDER THE **SAND** AT THE BOTTOM OF THE **SEA.** THE **ORGANS** DESIGNATED TO DETECT A CREATURE'S **ELECTRIC FIELD** ARE CALLED **AMPULLAE OF LORENZINI.**

THE **AMPULLAE** ARE
DISTRIBUTED MOSTLY
ON THE SHARK'S
SNOUT. THEY
ARE **SMALL
PORES** FILLED
WITH A
**GEL-LIKE
SUBSTANCE.**
INSIDE THE
GEL, THERE ARE
NERVE CELLS ABLE
TO DETECT **ELECTRIC FIELDS.**

AMPULLAE OF LORENZINI

N

W   E

S

IT'S POSSIBLE THAT SHARKS'
AMPULLAE OF LORENZINI ARE
ABLE TO SENSE THE **EARTH'S
MAGNETIC FIELD** FOR
ORIENTATION. BASICALLY, THE
AMPULLAE COULD FUNCTION AS A
COMPASS, HELPING SHARKS TO
NAVIGATE THROUGH **IMMENSE
OCEANS** WHERE **VISUAL
REFERENCES** ARE **RARE.**

LATERAL LINE

THE **LATERAL LINE** IS A **SENSE** THAT IS SHARED BY **MANY FISH,** NOT JUST BY **SHARKS.** THE **LATERAL LINE** IS MADE UP OF A **ROW** OF **TINY PORES,** CALLED **NEUROMASTS,** RUNNING ALONG THE **SIDES** OF A **SHARK.** THE **NEUROMASTS** DETECT EVERY LITTLE **MOVEMENT** OR **VIBRATION** OF THE **WATER.**

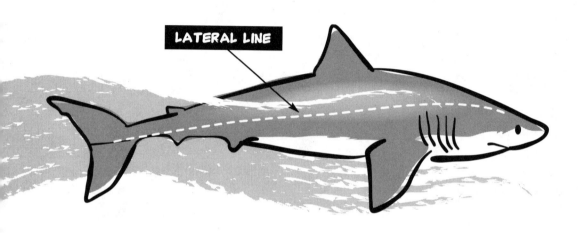

LATERAL LINE

WHEN SWIMMING, THE SHARK MAKES **SMALL WAVES** IN THE WATER. THESE WAVES HIT NEARBY **OBSTACLES,** ROCKS, OR OTHER FISH. LIKE AN **ECHO EFFECT,** THE WAVES **COME BACK** TO THE SHARK. THE SHARK'S LATERAL LINE **SENSES** THE **RETURNING WAVES,** AND AS A RESULT THE SHARK BECOMES MORE **AWARE** OF ITS **SURROUNDINGS.**

ANOTHER WAY THE **LATERAL LINE** HELPS SHARKS IS BY DETECTING THE **WAVES** MADE BY AN **INJURED** FISH. AN INJURED FISH IS OFTEN A SHARK'S **PERFECT PREY,** BECAUSE IT REQUIRES **LITTLE CHASE** AND **STRUGGLE.** INJURED FISH ARE **EASILY DETECTED** BY A SHARK'S LATERAL LINE BECAUSE THEY MOVE **ERRATICALLY** AND MAKE **UNEVEN WAVES** IN THE WATER.

IN AN **ENVIRONMENT** LIKE THE **OCEAN,** THE WATER IS NOT ALWAYS **CLEAR** AND THERE'S OFTEN NOT MUCH **LIGHT.** BOTH ITS **SIGHT** AND **LATERAL LINE** ARE VITAL **SENSES** A SHARK RELIES UPON TO DETECT ITS **SURROUNDINGS.**

SHARKS DON'T HAVE **EXTERNAL EARS** LIKE HUMANS, ONLY **INTERNAL ONES,** BUT THEY CAN HEAR **WELL.**

EARS

THE **INTERNAL HEARING ORGAN** IS CALLED **MACULA NEGLECTA** AND IS POSITIONED **INSIDE** THE SHARK'S **HEAD,** TOWARD THE TOP.

Shark Tales: Sharks and bony fish have a tongue that is very different from ours. It's called a basihyal. In most sharks, the basihyal is short, hard, and doesn't move around. It's not even used for taste!

SHARKS TASTE THROUGH **TASTE BUDS** LOCATED INSIDE THE **MOUTH** AND **THROAT,** BUT NOT ON THE TONGUE.

BARBELS

SOME SHARKS HAVE **NASAL BARBELS.** THEY ARE LOCATED **AROUND** THE **MOUTH** AND LOOK LIKE **WHISKERS.** NASAL BARBELS ARE VERY **SENSITIVE RECEPTORS** THAT COLLECT INFORMATION ABOUT **TASTE** AND **SMELL.**

SHARK SKIN

THE **SHARK'S SKIN** IS MADE OF **SMALL** AND **HARD SCALES** CALLED **PLACOIDS.** EACH PLACOID BEARS A VERY **SMALL, TOOTH-LIKE SPINE.** THESE ARE CALLED **DERMAL** (OR SKIN) **DENTICLES.** ALL THE DENTICLES **POINT** TOWARD THE **TAIL** OF THE SHARK. SO, THE SHARK'S SKIN IS **SMOOTH** FROM **HEAD** TO **TAIL,** BUT **VERY PRICKLY** FROM **TAIL** TO **HEAD.** SOME SHARKS HAVE **ROUGHER SKIN** THAN OTHERS.

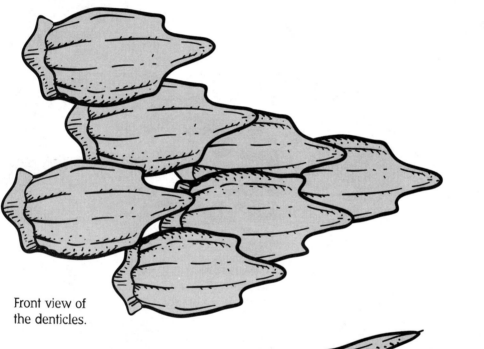

Front view of the denticles.

Side view.

Shark Tales: Leather made from sharks skin is extremely tough. It's used in the apparel industry to make leather goods such as wallets and belts.

BONY FISH ARE COVERED WITH **SCALES**. THE SCALES BECOME **BIGGER** AS THE FISH **GROWS** AND COULD EASILY BE **REMOVED**. THE SCALES REMAIN THE **SAME** IN **NUMBER** THROUGHOUT THE **LIFE** AND **GROWTH** OF THE FISH.

SHARK SKIN, ON THE OTHER HAND, IS VERY **TOUGH** AND THE **DENTICLES** ARE **ROOTED** IN IT. SHARKS' **PLACOIDS** DON'T **GROW** IN **SIZE** AS THE SHARK GROWS, INSTEAD THEY **MULTIPLY**.

Shark Tales: The water running through the denticles allows sharks to swim efficiently and silently. This is because there's very little friction between the water and the shark. For this reason, shark skin has been studied and emulated to create swimsuits for Olympic swimmers.

SHARK REPRODUCTION

SHARK EMBRYOS DEVELOP IN **ONE** OF **THREE WAYS**, DEPENDING ON THE **SHARK'S SPECIES**. SOME SHARKS LAY **EGGS** (THEY ARE **OVIPAROUS**), SOME **DELIVER PUPS** (THEY ARE **VIVIPAROUS**), AND FINALLY MOST SHARKS ARE A **COMBINATION** OF THE **TWO** (THEY ARE **OVOVIVIPAROUS**).

IN ALL THREE CASES, THE **EGGS** ARE FERTILIZED **INSIDE** THE **FEMALE SHARK'S BODY** DURING MATING. THIS IS NOT VERY **COMMON** IN BONY FISH. GENERALLY, THE FEMALE FISH FIRST **LAYS** THE **EGGS**, THEN THE MALE **FERTILIZES** THEM.

OVIPAROUS SHARKS

SOME SHARK SPECIES, LIKE **SWELL SHARKS** AND **CATSHARKS**, DEPOSIT **EGGS**. ONCE THE EGGS ARE **FERTILIZED** INSIDE THE FEMALE'S BODY, THEY ARE DEPOSITED AT THE **BOTTOM** OF THE **SEA**.

THE **SHAPE, SIZE,** AND **COLOR** OF THE EGGS DEPEND ON THE **SPECIES**. SOME EGGS HAVE **LITTLE HOOKS** AND **CURLS**. THE FEMALE SHARK **ATTACHES** THE **EGGS** TO **UNDERWATER PLANTS** OR **ROCKS**. THIS IS DONE SO THAT **PREDATORS** HAVE A HARD TIME **FINDING** AND **EATING** THEM.

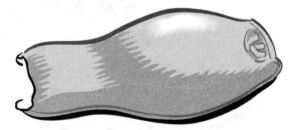

The swell shark's egg.

Egg yolk.

Egg shell.

Shark embryo.

An embryo developing inside the swell shark's egg.

Shark Tales: Because of their shape, some sharks' eggs are called "mermaid's purse."

The Port Jackson shark and its screw-shaped egg.

Catsharks' eggs have four hooks, called tendrils. The tendrils are used to "tie" the eggs to coral and algae.

THE **EGG** PROVIDES THE **EMBRYO** WITH **FOOD** AND **PROTECTION.** EGGS CONTAINS **YOLK,** THAT **NOURISHES** THE SHARK WHILE IT'S STILL **GROWING.** THE **SHELL** PROTECTS IT FROM **PREDATORS.** ONCE **HATCHED,** THE PUPS ARE FULLY ABLE TO **FEND** FOR **THEMSELVES.**

SHARK REPRODUCTION

VIVIPAROUS SHARKS

SOME SHARK SPECIES, LIKE **BASKING SHARKS**, **HAMMERHEAD SHARKS**, AND **LEMON SHARKS**, ARE VIVIPAROUS. **VIVIPARITY** IS THE NAME OF A WAY OF **REPRODUCTION** IN WHICH THE FEMALE **GIVES BIRTH** TO **PUPS**.

A **SHARK'S PUP** DEVELOPS **INSIDE** ITS **MOTHER'S BODY** AND IS **LINKED** TO THE MOTHER'S **PLACENTA** BY AN **UMBILICAL CORD.** THE PLACENTA IS A **TEMPORARY ORGAN** THAT PROVIDES **NOURISHMENT** TO THE **PUP.** IT ALSO PASSES OUT THE PUP'S **WASTE.**

A lemon shark has just given birth to its pup.

The basking shark is the second biggest shark.

JUST LIKE SHARKS, **HUMANS** AND **MOST MAMMALS** ARE **VIVIPAROUS.** UNLIKE SHARKS, HUMANS ARE **CARING PARENTS** AND **RAISE** THEIR **BABIES** FOR QUITE SOME TIME AFTER BIRTH. FOR SHARKS IT IS VERY DIFFERENT. ONCE DELIVERED, THE **PUPS** SWIM **QUICKLY AWAY** FROM THEIR MOTHER. THE MOTHER MIGHT ACTUALLY **EAT** THE PUPS THAT **LINGER,** THINKING THEY ARE **PREY.** ON THE OTHER HAND, SHARK PUPS ARE **FULLY ABLE** TO TAKE **CARE** OF THEMSELVES.

The great hammerhead shark is viviparous, too.

SHARK REPRODUCTION

OVOVIVIPAROUS SHARKS

OVOVIVIPARITY IS A **COMBINATION** BETWEEN **VIVIPARITY** AND **OVIPARITY**. THE **EGGS** ARE **FERTILIZED** INSIDE THE **MOTHER'S BODY,** WHERE THEY ALSO **HATCH.** BUT THE **SHARK PUPS** AREN'T **LINKED** TO THEIR MOTHER'S THROUGH A **PLACENTA.**

WHILE THEY REMAIN INSIDE THEIR MOTHER, THE **EMBRYOS** FEED ON THE **UNHATCHED EGGS** STILL PRESENT IN THEIR MOTHER'S **WOMB.** THE PRACTICE OF EATING UNHATCHED EGGS IS CALLED **OOPHAGY.** SOME SPECIES PROVIDE THEIR **UNBORN SHARKS** WITH A **NUTRIENT SUBSTANCE** CALLED **UTERINE MILK.**

THE **SANDTIGER SHARK'S EMBRYOS** PRACTICE A FORM OF **CANNIBALISM** CALLED **ADELPHOPHAGY**. AFTER HAVING **EATEN** ALL THE EGGS, THE **BIGGER SHARK PUPS** FEAST ON THEIR **SMALLER SIBLINGS**. THEY **EAT** THEM ALL UP, UNTIL GENERALLY ONLY **TWO SHARK PUPS** REMAIN AND ARE **DELIVERED**.

Sharks don't provide any parental care to their young.

THERE ARE **SEVERAL SPECIES** OF SHARKS WHOSE **EMBRYOS** ARE SUSPECTED OF PRACTICING **ADELPHOPHAGY**, LIKE THE **PELAGIC THRESHERS, SALMON SHARKS**, AND **MAKOS**.

A sandtiger shark with its surviving newborn pups.

PALEOZOIC ERA

CAMBRIAN PERIOD 543–490 MYA	ORDOVICIAN PERIOD 490–443 MYA	SILURAN PERIOD 443–417 MYA

ON LAND

SHARKS HAVE BEEN AROUND FOR MORE THAN **400 MILLION YEARS.** THEY FIRST APPEARED IN THE **OCEANS** OF THE **LATE ORDOVICIAN PERIOD.** BY THAT TIME, THE OCEANS WERE ALREADY **POPULATED** WITH **MANY KINDS** OF **FISH** AND MANY **INVERTEBRATES,** LIKE **SQUID** AND **MOLLUSKS.**

ON LAND, ON THE OTHER HAND, THERE WAS **NO SIGN** OF **ANIMAL LIFE.** EVEN THE **VEGETATION** WAS LIMITED TO **LICHENS** AND **FUNGI.**

DURING THE SILURAN PERIOD, **INSECTS** MADE THEIR FIRST APPEARANCE **ON LAND,** AT THE SAME TIME AS **FERNS** AND **HORSETAILS.**

Centipedes and ferns date as far back as the Siluran period.

IN THE SEA

THE **FIRST ANIMALS** WITH A **BACKBONE** WERE CALLED **VERTEBRATES** AND LIVED IN THE OCEANS. THEY WERE THE **AGNATA,** WHICH MEANS **"FISH WITHOUT JAWS."**

EARLY IN THIS PERIOD, THE **JAWED FISH** AROSE FROM THE AGNATA.

LATER, A NEW GROUP OF FISH CALLED **CHONDRICHTHYANS** EMERGED. THESE WERE THE FIRST **CARTILAGINOUS FISH,** THE **ANCESTORS** OF **SHARKS, RAYS,** AND **SKATES.**

Pikaia was an early jawless fish.

Cladoselache was one of the first sharks. It probably lived during the Siluran period.

DEVONIAN PERIOD 417–354 MYA	CARBONIFEROUS PERIOD 354–290 MYA	PERMIAN PERIOD 290–250 MYA

A **GROUP** OF **FISH** LEFT THE **WATERS** AND VENTURED ONTO **LAND**. THE **DESCENDANTS** OF THIS GROUP WERE THE **FIRST AMPHIBIANS**.

DURING THE CARBONIFEROUS PERIOD, **DRAGONFLIES** AND **COCKROACHES** APPEARED TOGETHER WITH THE **FIRST REPTILES**. THIS LAST GROUP DESCENDED FROM THE **AMPHIBIANS**.

THE **REPTILES** ORIGINATED THE **THEOCODONTS**. THEY WERE THE **ANCESTORS** OF **DINOSAURS**.

Compared to the many species living in the sea, the lands were bare until the arrival of amphibians.

STETHACANTHUS WAS A WEIRD-LOOKING **SHARK** OF THE DEVONIAN AND CARBONIFEROUS PERIODS. ITS **FIRST DORSAL FIN** WAS **FLAT** ON **TOP** AND WAS **COVERED** BY A LAYER OF **SPINES**. MORE SPINES WERE ON **TOP** OF STETHACANTHUS' **HEAD**.

XENACANTHUS WAS A **SHARK** THAT APPEARED IN THE CARBONIFEROUS PERIOD AND BECAME **EXTINCT** DURING THE PERMIAN. IT HAD A **LONG, THREATENING SPINE** ON ITS **HEAD**.

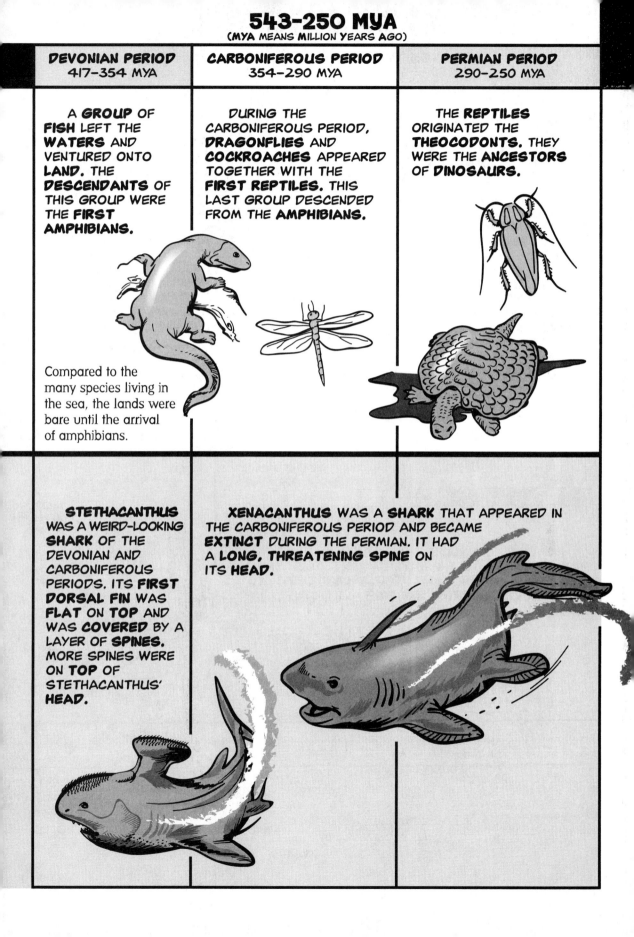

MESOZOIC ERA

| TRIASSIC PERIOD 250–206 MYA | JURASSIC PERIOD 206–144 MYA |

ON LAND

THE MESOZOIC ERA WAS ALSO CALLED **THE AGE OF REPTILES.** DURING THE TRIASSIC PERIOD, **DINOSAURS,** A SPECIAL KIND OF **REPTILE,** FIRST SHOWED UP ON **EARTH.**

Eoraptor is the earliest known dinosaur.

Stegasaurus was a dinosaur of the Jurassic period.

IN THE SEA

REPTILES CONQUERED THE **OCEANS,** TOO. THEY HAD TO **ADAPT** TO THE **ENVIRONMENT.** THEY GREW **FINS** FOR **SWIMMING,** AND **NEEDLE-LIKE TEETH** TO CATCH **SQUIRMY PREY,** LIKE FISH AND OCTOPI.

Elasmosaurus was a marine reptile and had a very long neck.

Ichthyosaurus looked like a dolphin, but was a marine reptile, too, like Elasmosaurus.

250-65 MYA
(MYA MEANS MILLION YEARS AGO)

CRETACEOUS PERIOD
144-65 MYA

Pterodactylus was a flying reptile of the Late Jurassic period.

The ferocious T. rex became extinct at the end of the Mesozoic Era.

WHEN **HYBODUS** WAS ALIVE, IT HAD TO **SHARE** ITS **ENVIRONMENT** WITH MANY **MARINE REPTILES**. THIS SHARK WAS A **CONTEMPORARY** OF THE **DINOSAURS**. HYBODUS BECAME **EXTINCT** AT THE END OF THE **CRETACEOUS PERIOD**. AT THE SAME TIME, ALL MARINE REPTILES, FLYING REPTILES, AND DINOSAURS BECAME **EXTINCT**, TOO.

CENOZOIC ERA

ON LAND

THE **CENOZOIC ERA** IS THE ONE IN WHICH WE ARE **LIVING**. IT STARTED **65 MILLION YEARS AGO** AFTER THE **K/T EVENT**. THE K/T EVENT WAS A **WORLDWIDE CATASTROPHE** THAT BROUGHT TO **EXTINCTION** NUMEROUS SPECIES, LIKE **DINOSAURS, MARINE** AND **FLYING REPTILES,** AND MANY OTHERS.

THE **FIRST HOMINIDS** APPEARED AT THE END OF THE **TERTIARY PERIOD**. HOMINIDS WERE THE **ANCESTORS** OF **HUMANS**. AT THE SAME TIME, IN THE **OCEANS,** AN **ENORMOUS SHARK** APPEARED. ITS **TEETH** WERE ALMOST **THREE TIMES** THE **SIZE** OF THAT OF A MODERN **GREAT WHITE SHARK.** FOR THIS REASON, IT WAS CALLED **"HUGE TOOTH,"** OR **MEGALODON.**

The Cenozoic Era is also known as "The Age of the Mammals." Many species, still alive today, first appeared during the Tertiary period.

IN THE SEA

Megalodon was a voracious shark that fed on marine mammals, like whales, dolphins, and seals.

Megalodon probably included Eurhinodelphis in its diet. Eurhinodelphis was an ancient whale.

Australopithecus was a hominid that lived about two million years ago.

Homo sapiens are our common ancestor. They lived in Africa about 150,000 years ago.

Mammoths and saber-tooth cats became extinct at the end of the Ice Age, 20,000 years ago.

And this is you today.

A seal.

A sea lion.

Not all sharks prey on seals and sea lions. Many sharks like to eat shellfish. Other sharks, like Megamouth, feed on zooplankton.

MEGALODON

"Huge Tooth"

MEGALODON WAS A **ENORMOUS SHARK** THAT EVOLVED IN THE **MIOCENE EPOCH,** 30 MILLION YEARS AGO. IT BECAME **EXTINCT** IN THE **PLEISTOCENE EPOCH,** 10,000 YEARS AGO.

Megalodon was big enough to hunt ancient whales!

MEGALODON WAS A **FIERCE PREDATOR** THAT FED ON **FISH,** OTHER **SHARKS,** AND **MARINE MAMMALS,** LIKE **SEALS, SEA LIONS,** AND **WHALES.** FOSSILIZED **MEGALODON TEETH** AND FOSSILIZED **BONES** OF **MARINE MAMMALS** HAVE OFTEN BEEN FOUND IN THE **SAME PLACES,** PROVING THAT THESE **ANIMALS** LIVED AT THE **SAME TIME.**

VERY LITTLE IS KNOWN OF **MEGALODON**. **CARTILAGE**, THE **SUBSTANCE** OF WHICH **SHARKS' SKELETONS** ARE MADE, DOESN'T **FOSSILIZE** LIKE REGULAR BONES. **FOSSILS OF SHARKS** ARE **RARE**. SO FAR, ONLY **FEW** OF MEGALODON **VERTEBRAE** HAVE BEEN **DISCOVERED**.

A great white shark's tooth.

A megalodon's tooth.

ON THE OTHER HAND, THERE ARE MANY **FOSSILIZED MEGALODON TEETH**. SHARKS SHED **THOUSANDS** OF **TEETH** DURING THEIR **LIFETIME**. TEETH ARE **COMPOSED** OF A **BONE-LIKE SUBSTANCE**, WHICH **FOSSILIZES WELL**.

Megalodon teeth were similar to the great white shark teeth, only much bigger.

MOST OF WHAT **PALEONTOLOGISTS** KNOW ABOUT **MEGALODON** WAS LEARNED FROM ITS **FOSSILIZED TEETH**. THEY NOTICED THAT **MEGALODON'S** AND THE **GREAT WHITE SHARK'S TEETH** ARE **SIMILAR**. ALTHOUGH MEGALODON'S TEETH WERE **BIGGER**, THEY WERE BOTH **TRIANGULAR** AND **SERRATED**. IT'S VERY LIKELY, THEN, THAT THESE TWO SHARKS' **LIFESTYLES** WERE **SIMILAR**, TOO.

GREAT WHITES' **FAVORITE FOOD** IS **FISH**, BUT THEY COME NEAR THE SHORES TO PREY UPON **SEALS** AND **SEA LIONS**. GREAT WHITES DON'T LIKE TO **VENTURE** INTO **WATERS** THAT ARE **TOO COLD**, BUT CAN **TRAVEL** THROUGH THE **OCEANS**. THESE AND MANY OTHER **CHARACTERISTICS** WERE PROBABLY SHARED BY MEGALODON. BUT BECAUSE IT WAS A **MUCH BIGGER SHARK**, ITS PREY WERE **BIGGER**, TOO.

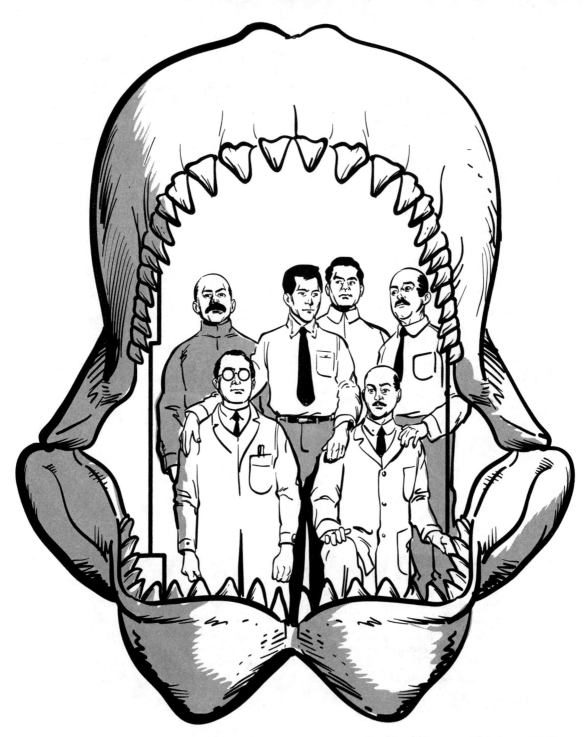

Bashford Dean and his team inside
the reconstructed jaws of megalodon.

IN 1909, PROFESSOR **BASHFORD DEAN** RECONSTRUCTED THE **JAWS** OF A **MEGALODON** FOR THE **MUSEUM OF NATURAL HISTORY** IN **NEW YORK.** NOTICING THE **TREMENDOUS DIFFERENCE** IN **SIZE** BETWEEN THE **TEETH** OF **MEGALODON** AND THAT OF A **GREAT WHITE,** DEAN ESTIMATED THAT **MEGALODON** COULD HAVE REACHED THE **EXTRAORDINARY LENGTH** OF **75 FEET!**

If megalodon was the size Dean had thought, this is how it would compare with a great white and a person.

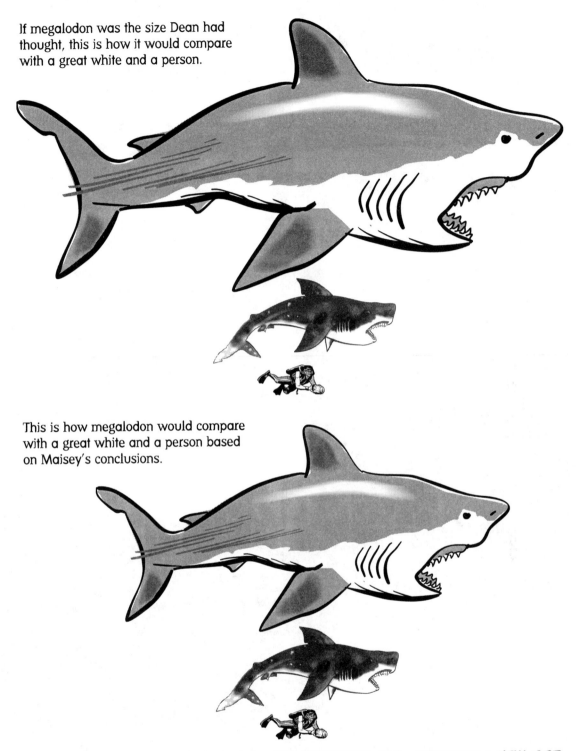

This is how megalodon would compare with a great white and a person based on Maisey's conclusions.

THE **SMITHSONIAN INSTITUTE** IN **WASHINGTON, D.C.,** EXHIBITED A **NEW SET** OF **MEGALODON JAWS** IN 1985. THE SMITHSONIAN HAD APPOINTED PALEONTOLOGIST **JOHN MAISEY** TO SUPERVISE THE **RECONSTRUCTION.** MAISEY BASED IT ON HIS OWN **STUDIES** AND ON **PETE HARMATUK'S RECENT FINDINGS.** HARMATUK, A **FOSSIL COLLECTOR,** HAD JUST **DISCOVERED** AN **ALMOST COMPLETE** SET OF MEGALODON TEETH!

MAYBE IT WAS DISAPPOINTING THAT THE **NEW SET** OF **JAWS** SUGGESTED THAT MEGALODON WASN'T AS **BIG** AS BASHFORD DEAN HAD BELIEVED. BUT, AT AN ESTIMATED **50 FEET** IN LENGTH, **MEGALODON** WAS PROBABLY THE **BIGGEST MEAT-EATING FISH** THAT EVER **EXISTED!**

MEGALODON LIVES!

ABOUT **10,000 YEARS AGO,** MEGALODON BECAME **EXTINCT.** ITS EXTINCTION WAS PROBABLY DUE TO CHANGES IN THE **ENVIRONMENT** TO WHICH MEGALODON WASN'T ABLE TO **ADAPT.** BUT SOME PEOPLE THINK THAT MEGALODON IS STILL **ALIVE!**

SOME PEOPLE CLAIM TO HAVE **SEEN** MEGALODON. THE **MOST FAMOUS REPORT** WAS BY RENOWNED WRITER **ZANE GREY** AND HIS SON **LOREN.** ON **TWO** DIFFERENT **OCCASIONS,** DURING FISHING TRIPS, **ZANE** AND **LOREN** SAW AN **UNKNOWN SHARK** EMERGING FROM THE **ABYSS.** ZANE AND LOREN WERE **FERVID FISHERMEN** AND HAD **SEEN** MANY **SHARKS.** NOT ABLE TO **RECOGNIZE** THIS ONE, THEY THOUGHT IT MUST HAVE BEEN **MEGALODON.**

DAVID STEAD, AN AUSTRALIAN NATURALIST, REPORTED ANOTHER **ENCOUNTER** WITH A **MYSTERIOUS FISH.** IT HAPPENED IN **1920,** WHEN SOME **FISHERMEN** SAW A **HUGE SHARK** DISRUPTING **CRAYFISH POTS** AND **FISHING LINES.** AS **STEAD** POINTED OUT, THESE MEN WERE AT SEA **EVERY DAY** AND KNEW **MANY KINDS** OF **SHARKS,** BUT WERE UNABLE TO **IDENTIFY** THIS ONE. COULD THE **MYSTERIOUS SHARK** HAVE BEEN **MEGALODON?**

DEPOSITS OF MANGANESE **DIOXIDE,** A MINERAL ON MEGALODON'S **TEETH,** APPEAR TO INDICATE THAT THIS SHARK LIVED **1,000 YEARS AGO.** THIS **MIGHT** SEEM A **LONG TIME,** BUT IT'S NOT SO IN **GEOLOGICAL TERMS.** THERE ARE **MANY ANIMAL SPECIES** THAT WERE ALIVE 1,000 YEARS AGO AND STILL **SURVIVE** TODAY.

IN 1976 A **NEW SHARK** WAS **DISCOVERED.** IT WAS THE **MEGAMOUTH SHARK.** MEGAMOUTH SHARKS CAN BE AS **BIG** AS **GREAT WHITES.** IT'S SURPRISING THAT SUCH A **BIG FISH** HAD GONE UNNOTICED BY SCIENTISTS FOR SO LONG! COULDN'T IT BE, THEN, THAT **MEGALODON** IS STILL **ALIVE** IN THE **DEPTHS** OF THE **OCEANS, WAITING** TO BE **DISCOVERED?**

MEGALODON IS DEAD!

THE **THEORY** THAT **MEGALODON** IS STILL **ALIVE** IS BASED ON **EYEWITNESS REPORTS**, STUDIES OF **TEETH**, AND THE **RECENT DISCOVERY** OF AN **UNKNOWN SHARK**, **MEGAMOUTH**. BUT FOR EVERY **CLAIM**, THERE SEEMS TO BE A **LOGICAL EXPLANATION!**

THE **AMOUNT** OF **DEPOSITS** OF **MANGANESE DIOXIDE** ON **FOSSILIZED MEGALODON'S TEETH** HAS MORE TO DO WITH THE **CHEMISTRY** OF THE **ENVIRONMENT** THAN WITH **TIME**. SO THIS PARTICULAR **MINERAL** CANNOT BE USED TO **DATE** FOSSILS.

THERE IS A **VERY GOOD CHANCE** THAT BOTH THE **ZANES'** AND THE **CRAWFISH MEN'S ACCOUNTS** WERE **EXAGGERATED**. THEY COULD HAVE GOTTEN **CARRIED AWAY** WHEN THEY DESCRIBED WHAT THEY HAD SEEN. THIS IS A **COMMON REACTION** WHEN PEOPLE **WITNESS** SOMETHING THAT **UPSETS** OR **SHOCKS** THEM.

IT'S TRUE THAT WE DON'T KNOW A LOT ABOUT THE **OCEANS**. SO FAR, **MEGAMOUTH SHARKS** HAVE BEEN **CAUGHT** FEWER THAN **30 TIMES**. THEY LIVE **DEEP** IN THE **OCEAN** AND DON'T COME **NEAR** THE **SHORES**. THEY ARE **NOCTURNAL** AND FEED ON **ZOOPLANKTON**.

BUT MEGALODON'S **TEETH** SEEM TO POINT OUT THAT ITS **ENVIRONMENT** AND **HABITS** WERE **SIMILAR** TO THOSE OF THE **GREAT WHITE**.

AS BIOLOGIST **BEN ROESCH** POINTS OUT, **GREAT WHITES** ARE SOMETIMES SEEN NEAR THE **SHORES** PREYING ON **SEALS**. BUT, SO FAR, NOBODY HAS EVER SEEN **MEGALODON!**

SO, IS MEGALODON STILL ALIVE?
YOU DECIDE!

Types of Sharks

THERE'S NO ANAL FIN.

THE BODY IS **FLAT,** LIKE A RAY, AND THE **MOUTH** IS AT **FRONT.**

THE BODY ISN'T **FLAT,** AND THE **MOUTH** IS UNDERNEATH.

THE **SNOUT** IS **LONG** AND LOOKS LIKE A **SAW.**

THE **SNOUT** IS **SHORT.**

THERE IS AN ANAL FIN.

THERE ARE **FIVE** GILL SLITS, AND **TWO** DORSAL FINS.

THERE ARE **SIX** OR **SEVEN** GILL SLITS, AND **ONE** DORSAL FIN.

THERE AREN'T ANY **SPINES** ON THE DORSAL FIN.

THERE ARE **SPINES** ON DORSAL FIN.

THE **MOUTH** EXTENDS **BEHIND** THE **EYES.**

THE **MOUTH** ENDS **BEFORE** THE **EYES.**

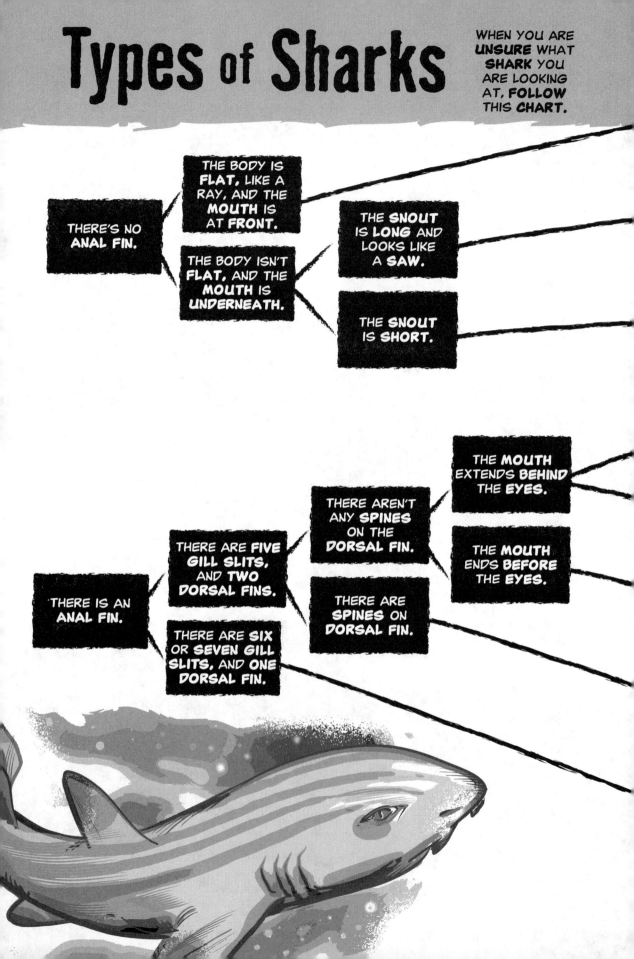

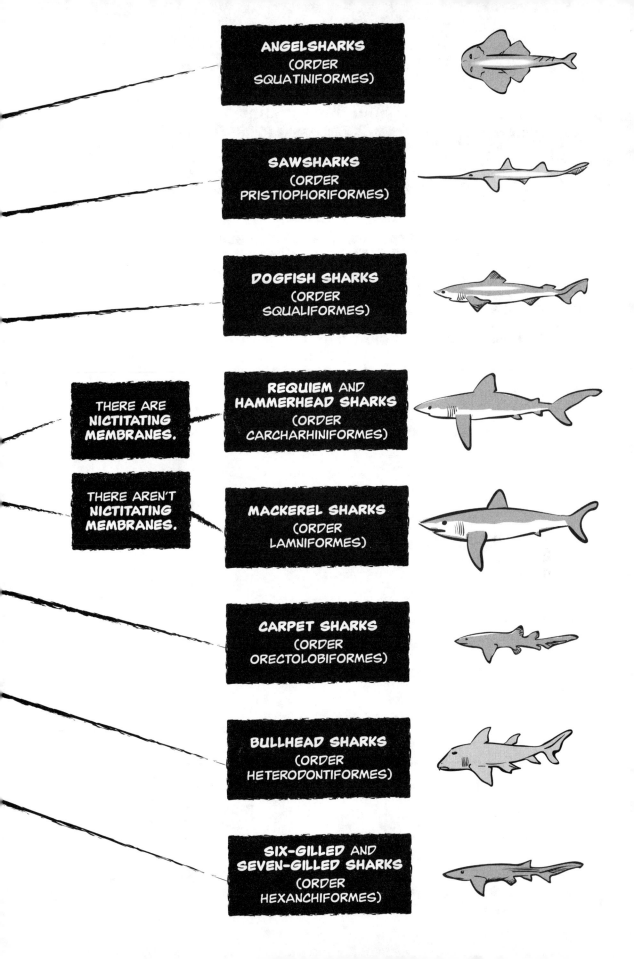

ANGELSHARKS
(ORDER SQUATINIFORMES)

SAWSHARKS
(ORDER PRISTIOPHORIFORMES)

DOGFISH SHARKS
(ORDER SQUALIFORMES)

THERE ARE NICTITATING MEMBRANES.

REQUIEM AND HAMMERHEAD SHARKS
(ORDER CARCHARHINIFORMES)

THERE AREN'T NICTITATING MEMBRANES.

MACKEREL SHARKS
(ORDER LAMNIFORMES)

CARPET SHARKS
(ORDER ORECTOLOBIFORMES)

BULLHEAD SHARKS
(ORDER HETERODONTIFORMES)

SIX-GILLED AND SEVEN-GILLED SHARKS
(ORDER HEXANCHIFORMES)

ANGELSHARK

Squatina squatina

Order Squatiniformes (Angelsharks)
Family Squatinidae (Angelsharks)

ANGELSHARKS ARE **BOTTOM-DWELLERS**. THEY **BURY** THEMSELVES IN THE **SAND** OR **MUD** OF THE **OCEAN FLOOR**, KEEPING OUT ONLY THEIR **EYES** AND PART OF THEIR **BACK**. THE **EYES** ARE **CONVENIENTLY LOCATED** ON **TOP** OF THEIR **HEAD**. THE **COLOR** OF THE **SKIN** HELPS THE ANGELSHARK'S **CAMOUFLAGE** ON THE **OCEAN FLOOR**. WHEN A **PREY** PASSES BY **UNAWARE**, THE ANGELSHARK **JUMPS OUT** FROM ITS **HIDING PLACE** AND **SNATCHES** IT.

An angelshark hiding under the sand.

THEIR **TEETH** ARE **VERY SHARP** AND **POINTY** TO BETTER CATCH **SLIPPERY PREY**, LIKE **SQUID** AND **RAYS**.

← SCALE →

Length: 6 feet

ANGELSHARKS ARE CAUGHT FOR **FOOD** IN MANY COUNTRIES **AROUND** THE **WORLD**. ANGELSHARKS' **PECTORAL FINS** CAN BE CUT INTO **STEAKS**.

THEY HAVE **LARGE PECTORAL FINS** THAT RESEMBLE THE **WINGS** OF A **RAY.** UNLIKE RAYS, THE **PECTORAL FINS** ARE **NOT ATTACHED** TO THE **HEAD,** BUT TO THE **SIDES** OF THE **BODY.**

ANGELSHARKS OWE THEIR NAME TO THEIR **PECTORAL FINS.** THEY ARE SO **WIDE,** THEY LOOK LIKE **WINGS.**

THEIR **FLESHY BARBELS** ON THEIR **SNOUTS** HELP THEM SENSE THEIR **PREY HIDING** IN THE **SAND.**

THE **BODY** OF THE ANGELSHARK IS **VERY FLAT.**

ANGELSHARKS HAVE **TWO DORSAL FINS** AND NO **ANAL FIN.** THE **LOWER LOBE** OF THE ANGELSHARK'S TAIL IS **LONGER** THAN THE **UPPER LOBE.**

ANGELSHARKS ARE **OVOVIVIPAROUS.** THE AVERAGE **LITTER** YIELDS UP TO **20 PUPS.**

ANGELSHARK

ANGELSHARKS HAVE **TWO SPIRACLES** ON **TOP** OF THE **HEAD.** ANGELSHARKS **BREATHE** BOTH THROUGH THEIR **GILL SLITS** AND THROUGH THEIR **SPIRACLES.**

WHAT THEY EAT

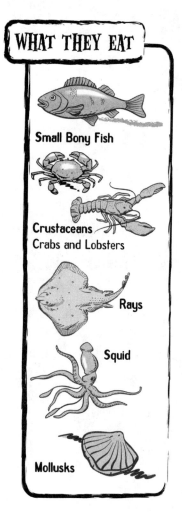

Small Bony Fish

Crustaceans
Crabs and Lobsters

Rays

Squid

Mollusks

BESIDES SWIMMING, ANGELSHARKS CAN ALSO **CRAWL** ON THE **SEA FLOOR** BY **UNDULATING** THEIR **PECTORAL FINS.**

THEY HAVE **FIVE GILL SLITS** UNDER THEIR **BODIES.**

PLINY THE ELDER, AN ANCIENT ROMAN NATURAL PHILOSOPHER, AND **ARISTOTLE,** AN ANCIENT GREEK PHILOSOPHER, BELIEVED THAT THE **ASHES** OF **ANGELSHARKS** COULD CURE **SKIN DISEASES.**

WHERE THEY LIVE

DEPENDING ON THE SPECIES, THEY CAN BE FOUND AT DEPTHS OF 10 TO **4,000 FEET.**

ANGELSHARKS ARE ALSO CALLED **MONKFISH,** BECAUSE THEIR **PECTORAL FINS** LOOK LIKE THE **COWL** OF A **MONK.** SOMETIMES THEY ARE CALLED **SAND DEVILS,** BECAUSE THEY **HIDE** UNDER THE **SAND** AND, WHEN THEY ARE **CAUGHT,** THEY CAN **HURT** THE **FISHERMEN** WITH THEIR **SPINES** AND **TEETH.**

SHARK BITEs!

1. HOW DO SHARKS **WEIGH THEMSELVES?**

–THEY USE **FISH SCALES!**

2. WHAT DO YOU CALL A **WHALE** THAT **WEARS PANTS?**

–A **BREACHED** WHALE!

3. WHAT DOES A **SHARK** SAY IN **COURT?**

–THE **TOOTH,** THE WHOLE **TOOTH,** AND NOTHING BUT THE **TOOTH!**

SIXGILL SAWSHARK

Pliotrema warreni

Order Pristiophoriformes (Sawsharks)
Family Pristiophoridae (Sawsharks)

THE **NAME** OF THIS **FAMILY** OF **SHARKS** IS COMPOSED OF TWO GREEK WORDS. **PRISTIO** MEANS "SAW," AND **PHORIDAE** MEANS "BEARER." ALL THE SHARKS OF THIS ORDER BEAR A **VERY LONG SNOUT** IN THE **SHAPE** OF A **SAW.**

SOMETIMES THESE SHARKS **WANDER** INTO **ESTUARIES.**

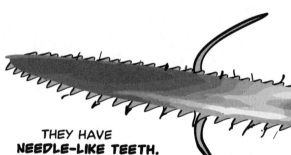

THEY HAVE **NEEDLE-LIKE TEETH.**

THIS SHARK HAS **SIX GILL SLITS.** OTHER SAWSHARKS IN THIS FAMILY ONLY HAVE **FIVE.**

WHAT THEY EAT

Small Bony Fish

Crustaceans

Cephalopods like Squid

SAWSHARKS RESEMBLE **SAWFISH**, WITH THEIR **LONG, FLAT,** AND **TOOTHED SNOUT.** UNLIKE SAWFISH, SAWSHARKS HAVE **TWO BARBELS** ON BOTH **SIDES** OF THE **SNOUT.**

← SCALE →

SAWSHARKS ARE **CAUGHT** FOR **FOOD.**

THEIR **LITTERS** YIELD ON AVERAGE **TEN PUPS.**

WHERE THEY LIVE

Length: 5 feet

LONGNOSE SAWSHARK

Pristiophorus cirratus

Order Pristiophoriformes (Sawsharks)
Family Pristiophoridae (Sawsharks)

SAWSHARKS HAVE
NO ANAL FINS.

THERE ARE **FIVE**
GILL SLITS ON **EACH**
SIDE OF THE **HEAD.**

WHERE THEY LIVE

←SCALE→

DESPITE THEIR **SHARP TEETH,** SAWSHARKS AREN'T **AGGRESSIVE.**

SAWSHARKS HAVE **TWO SPIRACLES** TO HELP THEM **BREATHE.**

ALL **SAWSHARKS** HAVE THEIR **MOUTHS** UNDER THEIR **HEADS.**

LONGNOSE SAWSHARKS LIVE ON **SANDY BOTTOMS.**

THE **SAWSHARK'S BARBELS** ARE **EXTREMELY SENSITIVE.** WHEN SAWSHARKS SCOUR THE **SEA FLOOR,** THE BARBELS ARE ABLE TO DETECT **PREY** HIDING IN THE **MUD.**

SAWSHARKS ARE **OVOVIVIPAROUS,** WHICH MEANS THAT THEY **GIVE BIRTH** TO **LIVE YOUNG,** AS OPPOSED TO **LAYING EGGS.**

THE **TEETH** OF A **NEWBORN SAWSHARK** ARE **FLAT** AGAINST ITS **SNOUT.** IN THIS WAY, THE **PUP** DOESN'T **HURT** THE **MOTHER** BEFORE AND DURING **BIRTH.**

Length: 4.5 feet

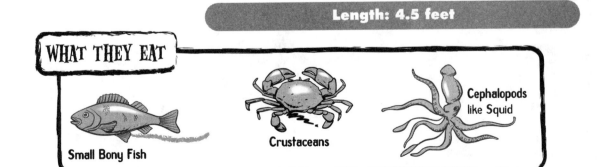

WHAT THEY EAT

Small Bony Fish

Crustaceans

Cephalopods like Squid

SHARK Q&A

WHICH IS THE BIGGEST SHARK?

It's the whale shark, which measures on average 65 feet in length!

WHICH IS THE SMALLEST?

It's the spine pygmy shark, only six inches long!

SHARK Q & A

DO SHARKS EAT PEOPLE?

Although humans have been attacked and eaten, a shark's regular diet does not include people.

WHICH ARE THE MOST DANGEROUS SHARKS?

The sharks that have been responsible for the most unprovoked attacks on people are the great white shark, the bull shark, and the tiger shark.

How Do Sharks Breathe?

SHARKS DON'T BREATHE **AIR** AND DON'T HAVE **LUNGS**. THEIR **NOSTRILS** ARE **CONNECTED** ONLY TO THEIR **BRAIN**. SHARKS USE THEIR NOSTRILS TO **DETECT ODORS**, NOT TO BREATHE.

A shortfin mako shark.

TO BREATHE, SHARKS LET **WATER** INTO THEIR **MOUTHS**. THE WATER GOES THROUGH THE **GILLS**, WHERE THE **OXYGEN** PRESENT IN THE WATER IS **EXTRACTED**. THEN, THE WATER IS **PUMPED OUT** FROM THE **GILL SLITS**. IN THE **GILLS**, THERE ARE MANY **BLOOD VESSELS** THAT **CAPTURE** THE **OXYGEN**. THE **HEART** PUMPS THE **OXYGEN-RICH BLOOD** THROUGHOUT THE **SHARK'S BODY**.

A bull shark.

A great hammerhead shark.

SOME SHARKS HAVE TO **CONSTANTLY SWIM** TO ALLOW **WATER** INTO THEIR **MOUTHS** AND OUT OF THEIR **GILLS**. THIS **METHOD** OF **BREATHING** IS CALLED **RAM-VENTILATION**. IF THESE SHARKS WEREN'T **SWIMMING**, THEY WOULDN'T BE ABLE TO **BREATHE**, AND THEY WOULD ALSO **SINK**. THESE **SPECIES** GENERALLY INCLUDE **SHARKS** THAT ARE **VERY ACTIVE**, LIKE **SHORTFIN MAKOS**, **GREAT WHITES**, AND **HAMMERHEAD SHARKS**.

A swell shark.

OTHER SHARKS ARE ABLE TO ACTIVELY **SUCK WATER** INTO THEIR **MOUTHS** AND **OUT** OF THEIR **GILLS**. THEY ARE **NOT OBLIGED** TO **CONSTANTLY SWIM** IN ORDER TO **BREATHE**. THESE SPECIES INCLUDE MORE **SLUGGISH, BOTTOM-DWELLER SHARKS**, LIKE **WOBBEGONGS** AND **SWELLSHARKS**.

A whitetip reef shark.

SOME SHARK SPECIES, LIKE **WHITETIP REEF SHARKS** AND **LEMON SHARKS**, ARE KNOWN TO **CONGREGATE** IN **LARGE NUMBERS** IN CAVES. ALTHOUGH THESE ARE **ACTIVE SHARKS**, THEY ARE ABLE TO **PUMP** IN **WATER** TO **BREATHE** WHEN THEY DON'T SWIM.

MANY SHARKS, ESPECIALLY **BOTTOM-DWELLERS**, HAVE **SPIRACLES** ON TOP OF THEIR **HEADS**. SPIRACLES **AID** THE SHARK IN THE **BREATHING PROCESS**. WHEN THEY **BURY** THEMSELVES IN THE **SAND** OR **LIE** ON THE **OCEAN FLOOR**, SHARKS **CAN'T BREATHE** THROUGH THEIR **GILLS**. IN THESE CASES, THE **WATER** ENTERS THROUGH THE **SPIRACLES**, INSTEAD OF THE **MOUTH**, AND IS **DELIVERED** TO THE **GILLS**.

A blind shark.

BRAMBLE SHARK

Echinorhinus brucus

Order Squaliformes (Dogfish Sharks)
Family Echinorhinidae (Bramble Sharks)

THIS SHARK IS NAMED **BRAMBLE SHARK** BECAUSE ITS **SKIN** IS COVERED WITH **PATCHES** OF **SPINES**. BRAMBLE SHARKS ARE VERY **PRICKLY**.

THE **SKIN COLOR** IS DARK BROWNISH-PURPLE, FADING TO A **LIGHTER BROWN** ON THE **BELLY**. THERE ARE ALSO **DARKER PATCHES** OF **PURPLE** ON THE **BACK**.

THERE'S ONLY THE **PELVIC FIN**, AND NO **ANAL FIN**.

IT CAN HAVE **LITTERS** OF **20 PUPS.**

THE BODY IS **SHORT** AND **SOFT.**

IT'S A **FAT** AND **SLOW-MOVING SHARK** BECAUSE IT LIVES IN **DEEP WATERS,** AT ABOUT **3,000 FEET.**

THE BRAMBLE SHARK DOESN'T HAVE ANY **SPINES** ON ITS **BACK.** OTHER **SHARKS** OF THIS **GROUP** HAVE **SPINES.**

THE BRAMBLE SHARK IS **COVERED** WITH **MUCUS** THAT **SMELLS AWFUL.**

Length: 7 feet

WHAT THEY EAT

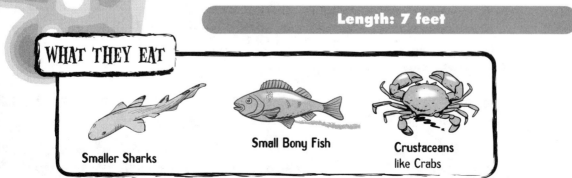

Smaller Sharks

Small Bony Fish

Crustaceans like Crabs

PIKED DOGFISH

Squalus acanthias

Order Squaliformes (Dogfish Sharks)
Family Squalidae (Dogfish Sharks)

PIKED DOGFISH ARE ONE OF THE **MOST COMMON SHARKS** AND ONE OF WHICH SCIENTISTS **KNOW THE MOST.**

IT PREFERS **WATERS** THAT ARE **45°** TO **50° FAHRENHEIT.**

PIKED DOGFISH ARE CAUGHT FOR **FOOD.** THEY ARE CALLED **ROCK SALMON** OR **FLAKE.**

PIKED DOGFISH LIKE TO FORM **BIG SCHOOLS.** THEY **SEGREGATE** BY **GENDER** AND **SIZE.** PREGNANT FEMALES STAY **CLOSER** TO THE **COASTS,** WHERE THEY **GATHER** TO **GIVE BIRTH.** MALES PREFER **DEEPER WATERS.**
SEGREGATION PREVENTS **CANNIBALISM. PIKED DOGFISH MALES** AND **NON-PREGNANT FEMALES** ATTACK AND EAT **PUPS** THAT **WANDER** TOO FAR FROM THE **COASTS!**

PIKED DOGFISH HAVE A LONG GESTATION PERIOD, **24 MONTHS!** THIS IS **LONGER** THAN THE GESTATION PERIOD OF **ELEPHANTS** AND **WHALES.**

THE **SKIN IS BROWNISH-GREY,** FADING TO **WHITE** ON THE BELLY. **JUVENILES** HAVE **SMALL WHITE DOTS** ON THEIR BACKS THAT **DISAPPEAR** WITH AGE.

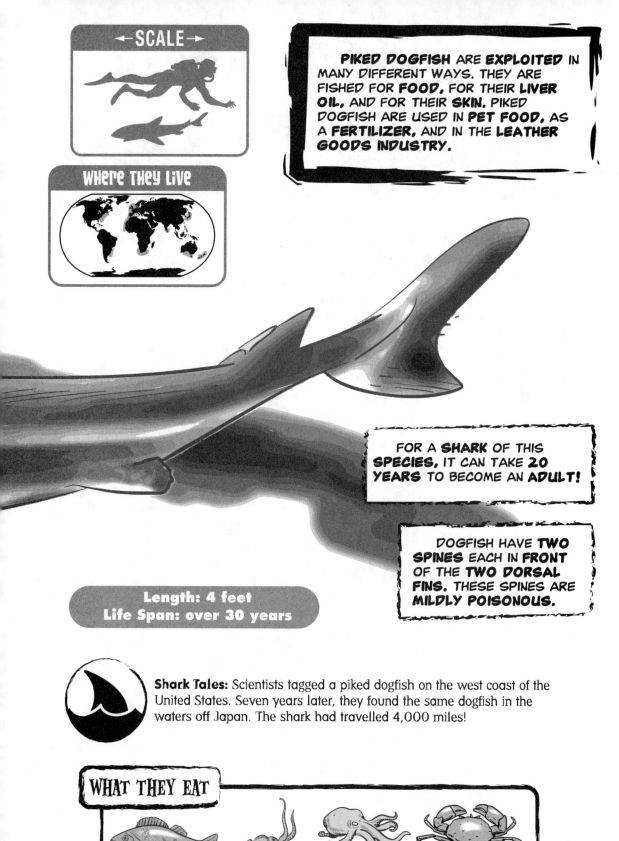

SCALE

WHERE THEY LIVE

PIKED DOGFISH ARE **EXPLOITED** IN MANY DIFFERENT WAYS. THEY ARE FISHED FOR **FOOD**, FOR THEIR **LIVER OIL**, AND FOR THEIR **SKIN**. PIKED DOGFISH ARE USED IN **PET FOOD**, AS A **FERTILIZER**, AND IN THE **LEATHER GOODS INDUSTRY**.

FOR A **SHARK** OF THIS **SPECIES**, IT CAN TAKE **20 YEARS** TO BECOME AN **ADULT**!

DOGFISH HAVE **TWO SPINES** EACH IN **FRONT** OF THE **TWO DORSAL FINS**. THESE SPINES ARE **MILDLY POISONOUS**.

Length: 4 feet
Life Span: over 30 years

Shark Tales: Scientists tagged a piked dogfish on the west coast of the United States. Seven years later, they found the same dogfish in the waters off Japan. The shark had travelled 4,000 miles!

WHAT THEY EAT

Bony Fish

Squid

Octopi

Crustaceans
Crabs and Shrimp

GREENLAND SHARK

Scymnodon squamulosus

Order Squaliformes (Dogfish Sharks)
Family Squalidae (Dogfish Sharks)

THE **GREENLAND SHARK** AND THE OTHER **SHARKS** OF THIS **FAMILY** CAN SWIM IN **DEEP WATERS**, DOWN TO **4,000 FEET**. FOR THIS REASON THEY ARE VERY **SLOW-MOVING SHARKS**. THAT'S WHY THEY ARE COMMONLY NAMED "**SLEEPERS**," A TRANSLATION OF THEIR LATIN NAME **SOMNIOSUS**.

THE GREENLAND SHARK OFTEN HAS **PARASITES** LIVING IN ITS **EYES.** THE **PARASITES** ARE **CRUSTACEANS,** AND ARE **VERY LONG.** THE GREENLAND SHARK USES THEM AS **BAIT.** FISH SWIM **CLOSE** TO THE GREENLAND SHARK TRYING TO **EAT** THE **PARASITES.** BUT THE **FISH** END UP **BEING EATEN** BY THE **GREENLAND SHARK!**

PARASITES FEED OFF THE GREENLAND SHARK'S **EYES,** CAUSING **SEVERE DAMAGE** AND EVENTUALLY LEADING TO **BLINDNESS!**

GREENLAND SHARKS' **PARASITES** ARE SO BIG THAT THEY HAVE **PARASITES,** TOO!

GREENLAND SHARKS DON'T SEEM TO **MIND** BEING **BLIND.** THEIR **SENSE** OF **SIGHT** ISN'T **VITAL** AND THEY **SURVIVE** RELYING ON THEIR **OTHER SENSES.**

GREENLAND SHARK

THE **MEAT** OF A **GREENLAND SHARK** IS **POISONOUS** UNLESS **PROPERLY COOKED.** PEOPLE WHO EAT IT RAW GET **FOOD POISONING.** THE **SYMPTOMS** RESEMBLE **DRUNKENNESS.** THE **INUIT PEOPLE'S WORD** FOR BEING DRUNK MEANS **"SHARK-SICK."**

THE **INUITS** ARE ABLE TO **COOK GREENLAND SHARK MEAT** SO THAT IT CAN BE **SAFELY EATEN.** THE DISH IS CALLED **HAKALL.**

Length: 20 feet

Shark Tales: A Greenland shark was found with a whole reindeer in its stomach!

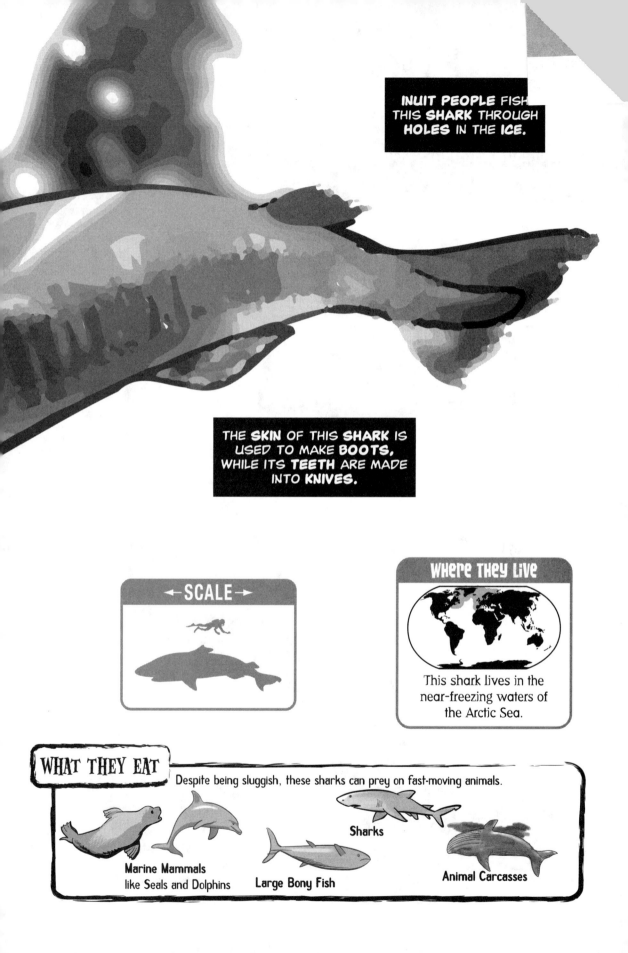

INUIT PEOPLE FISH THIS **SHARK** THROUGH **HOLES** IN THE **ICE.**

THE **SKIN** OF THIS **SHARK** IS USED TO MAKE **BOOTS**, WHILE ITS **TEETH** ARE MADE INTO **KNIVES.**

← SCALE →

WHERE THEY LIVE

This shark lives in the near-freezing waters of the Arctic Sea.

WHAT THEY EAT

Despite being sluggish, these sharks can prey on fast-moving animals.

Marine Mammals like Seals and Dolphins

Large Bony Fish

Sharks

Animal Carcasses

PYGMY SHARK

Euprotomicrus bispinatus

Order Squaliformes (Dogfish Sharks)
Family Squalidae (Dogfish Sharks)

THE **PYGMY SHARK** STALKS ITS PREY SWIMMING **UNDER** IT. THEN, IT **DASHES** TO **GRAB** IT. ITS **VICTIMS** ARE **UNAWARE** OF ITS **PRESENCE** BECAUSE THE PYGMY SHARK'S **BELLY** IS **LUMINESCENT.** WHEN **SEEN FROM ABOVE,** THIS SHARK DOESN'T **CAST** A **SHADOW.** ITS VICTIMS SEE IT COMING ONLY WHEN IT'S **TOO LATE!**

WHERE THEY LIVE

← SCALE →

THIS IS ONE OF THE **SMALLEST SHARKS,** ONLY **NINE INCHES LONG!**

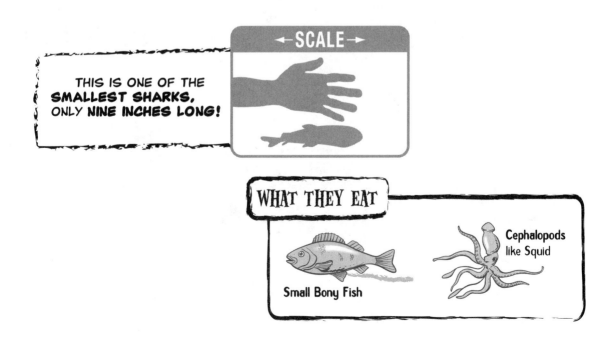

WHAT THEY EAT

Small Bony Fish

Cephalopods like Squid

CARIBBEAN LANTERNSHARKS

Etmopterus hillianus

Order Squaliformes (Dogfish Sharks)
Family Etmopteridae (Lanternsharks)

ALL **LANTERNSHARKS** HAVE SOME PART OF THEIR **BODIES** COVERED WITH A **MUCUS** THAT **GLOWS** IN THE **DARK.** THIS **PHENOMENON** IS CALLED **BIOLUMINESCENCE.** IT'S USED BY SHARKS THAT LIVE IN **DEEP WATERS,** WHERE **LIGHT** IS **SCARCE,** TO **ATTRACT** THEIR **PREY.**

LANTERNSHARKS HAVE **TWO SPIKES,** ONE IN FRONT OF EACH OF THEIR **DORSAL FINS.**

WHERE THEY LIVE

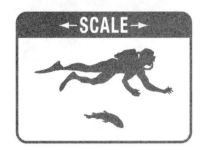

LANTERNSHARKS HAVE **TWO DORSAL FINS,** THE **FIRST** ONE WELL BEFORE THE **ANAL FIN.**

THE **CARIBBEAN LANTERNSHARK** HAS **SPOTS** ON ITS **HEAD** THAT **GLOW** IN THE **DARK.**

WHAT THEY EAT

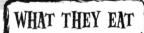

Small Bony Fish

Cephalopods like Squid

Very little is known about the diet of the Caribbean lanternshark. Other sharks of this family prey on small bony fish and squid, so it is thought that Caribbean lanternsharks do, too.

KITEFIN SHARK

Dalatias licha

Order Squaliformes (Dogfish Sharks)
Family Squalidae (Dogfish Sharks)

KITEFIN SHARK FEMALES ARE **BIGGER** THAN **MALES**. THE **FEMALES** ARE ABOUT **FIVE** AND **A HALF FEET LONG**, WHILE MALES DON'T GROW LONGER THAN **FOUR FEET**.

THE **SKIN COLOR** IS **DARK BROWN**, SOMETIMES **PURPLE**.

THE **UPPER TEETH** ARE **THIN** AND **SHARP**. THE **BOTTOM TEETH** ARE **TRIANGULAR** AND **SERRATED**. THE **UPPER TEETH** ARE USED TO **PIERCE** AND **HOLD** THE **PREY**, WHILE THE BOTTOM TEETH **CUT** THROUGH IT.

Length: males, 4 feet; females, 5.5 feet

←SCALE→

WHERE THEY LIVE

THE **SKIN** OF THE **KITEFIN SHARK** IS SO **ROUGH** THAT IT WAS USED BY **CABINETMAKERS** TO **SAND WOOD** AND TO **POLISH JEWELRY.** SHARK SKIN USED AS SANDPAPER IS CALLED SHAGREEN.

KITEFIN SHARK SKIN IS ALSO USED IN THE **LEATHER GOODS INDUSTRY.** IN **SPAIN,** THE LEATHER FROM THIS SHARK IS CALLED **BOROSO** AND IT'S **VERY EXPENSIVE.**

THE **LEATHER** FROM **KITEFIN SHARK SKIN** IS **MORE ELASTIC** AND **RESISTANT** THAN THE LEATHER MADE FROM **COW HIDE.**

KITEFIN SHARKS DON'T HAVE **ANAL FINS.**

THESE SHARKS HAVE **LITTERS** OF UP TO **15 PUPS.**

WHAT THEY EAT

Squid

Rays

Small Bony Fish

Crabs

Lobsters

Smaller Sharks

COOKIE-CUTTER SHARK

Isistius brasiliensis

Order Squaliformes (Dogfish Sharks)
Family Squalidae (Dogfish Sharks)

THE SCIENTIFIC NAME OF THIS SHARK IS **ISISTIUS BRASILIENSIS.** THE GENUS NAME COMES FROM **ISIS,** THE **EGYPTIAN GODDESS** OF **LIGHT.** THE NAME WAS CHOSEN BECAUSE THE COOKIE-CUTTER SHARK **GLOWS** IN THE **DARK.**

→ SCALE ←

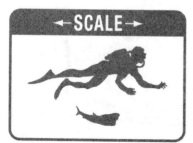

A COOKIE-CUTTER SHARK CAN **GLOW** IN THE **DARK** FOR **THREE HOURS** AFTER **DYING.**

Length: 2 feet

COOKIE-CUTTER SHARKS ARE **VERTICAL MIGRATORS.** THIS MEANS THAT, DURING THE **DAY,** THEY SWIM IN THE DEEP OCEAN, AT **11,000 FEET.** AT **NIGHT,** THEY COME **CLOSER** TO THE **SURFACE,** AT **ABOUT 300 FEET.**

EVERY DAY, IN THEIR **VERTICAL MIGRATION,** COOKIE-CUTTER SHARKS SWIM FOR ABOUT **TWO MILES.**

THE COOKIE-CUTTER SHARK HAS **TWO FINS** ON ITS **BACK,** VERY CLOSE TO ITS **TAIL.** THE FINS DON'T BEAR ANY **SPINES.** COOKIE-CUTTER SHARKS HAVE NO **ANAL FINS.** THE SKIN COLOR IS **DARKER BROWN** ON **TOP** AND **LIGHTER BROWN** ON THE **BELLY.** THEY HAVE A **DARK RING** AROUND THEIR **NECKS.**

COOKIE-CUTTER SHARKS ARE **NOCTURNAL.** THIS MEANS THAT THEY **HUNT** AT **NIGHT.**

COOKIE-CUTTER SHARK

A cookie-cutter shark attacking a wahoo.

The mark left by the cookie-cutter shark on the flank of the wahoo.

THE **COOKIE-CUTTER SHARK** ACTS LIKE A **PARASITE.** IT CHOOSES A **VICTIM** AND **ATTACHES** ITSELF TO IT WITH ITS **MOUTH,** USING ITS **LIPS** LIKE A **SUCTION CUP.** THEN, IT **QUICKLY ROTATES** ITS **BODY,** AND, WITH ITS **SHARP** AND **HUGE TEETH,** CUTS A **ROUND CHUNK** OFF OF ITS VICTIM.

COOKIE-CUTTER SHARKS LEAVE A **VERY RECOGNIZABLE MARK** ON THEIR **PREY.** THE MARK IS ABOUT **TWO INCHES ACROSS** AND **FOUR INCHES DEEP!** THE SHAPE OF THE MARK LOOKS LIKE THE **HOLE** THAT A **COOKIE-CUTTER** LEAVES IN **COOKIE DOUGH.**

THE **BELLY** OF THIS SHARK **GLOWS** IN THE **DARK**, EXCEPT FOR THE **DARKER CIRCLE** AROUND ITS **NECK**. WHEN VIEWED FROM **UNDERNEATH**, THE **DARK PATCH** ON ITS NECK LOOKS LIKE A **SMALL FISH** AGAINST THE **SOFT GLOW** OF ITS BELLY. THIS FAKE FISH **LURES** PREDATORS THAT **MISTAKE** IT FOR A **SMALL PREY**. WHEN A **PREDATOR** IS **CLOSE ENOUGH**, THE COOKIE-CUTTER SHARK **TURNS AGAINST** IT, **ATTACKS** IT, AND **BITES** IT, LEAVING ITS **DISTINCTIVE, ROUND MARK.**

 Shark Tales: Cookie-cutter sharks have bitten chunks off the neoprene protection of the radar domes of U.S. submarines. Nobody knows why these sharks are attracted to neoprene.

WHERE THEY LIVE

COOKIE-CUTTER SHARKS ARE OVOVIVIPAROUS.

SHARKS ARE KNOWN FOR **SHEDDING** AND **REPLACING** THEIR **TEETH**. BUT COOKIE-CUTTER SHARKS **RECYCLE** THEM! INSTEAD OF LETTING THEM **FALL OFF**, THEY **SWALLOW** AND **DIGEST** THEM. THIS IS PROBABLY DONE BECAUSE **TEETH** ARE **RICH** IN **CALCIUM** AND OTHER MINERALS.

WHAT THEY EAT

Cookie-cutter sharks attach themselves and bite chunks out of very large prey, too large to be eaten whole. They also eat small prey.

Marine Mammals like Dolphins, Porpoises, and Whales.

Bigger Sharks

Large Bony Fish like Tuna

Squid

Small Bony Fish

Crustaceans

PRICKLY DOGFISH

Oxynotus bruniensis

Order Squaliformes (Dogfish Sharks)
Family Oxynotidae (Roughsharks)

NOT MUCH IS KNOWN ABOUT THIS SHARK. THE **SPIRACLES** AND THE **BODY SHAPE** LEAD SCIENTISTS TO THINK THAT THE **PRICKLY DOGFISH** LIVES NEAR THE **BOTTOM** OF THE **OCEAN**, FEEDING ON **INVERTEBRATES** AND **SMALL BONY FISH**.

THE **COLOR** OF THE **SKIN** IS **BROWN** AND **GREY**. THE **DORSAL FINS** ARE **WHITE**.

THE **SECOND DORSAL FIN** IS ALIGNED WITH THE **PELVIC FIN**.

WHAT THEY EAT

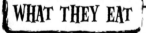

Small Bony Fish

Invertebrates
Worms and Snails

THIS **FAMILY** OF SHARKS HAVE A PARTICULARLY **ROUGH SKIN**.

← SCALE →

WHERE THEY LIVE

THE **SHARKS** BELONGING TO THE **OXYNOTIDAE FAMILY** HAVE A **DISTINCTIVE BODY SHAPE.** THIS IS **DIFFERENT** FROM THE **OTHER SHARKS** OF THE SAME **ORDER SQUALIFORMES.** THEIR BODY SHAPE IS MORE **SAUSAGE-LIKE,** TAPERED ON BOTH ENDS.

A prickly dogfish.

A piked dogfish.

ROUGHSHARKS HAVE **TWO DORSAL FINS** IN THE **SHAPE** OF A **SAIL.** THE **FIRST DORSAL FIN** IS VERY **BIG.** THERE ARE **TWO SPINES** IN **FRONT** OF EACH OF THE **DORSAL FINS.** THE **FIRST SPINE** POINTS **FORWARD.**

THE WORD **OXYNOTUS** MEANS "**HUMPED BACK,**" AND REFERS TO THE **BODY SHAPE** OF THIS SHARK.

THE BODY IS **STOUT** AND THERE ARE **TWO MARKED CREASES** ALONG THE **SIDES.**

THEY LIVE AT **DEPTHS** RANGING BETWEEN **150** AND **2,000 FEET.**

PRICKLY DOGFISH HAVE **LITTERS** OF FEWER THAN **TEN PUPS.**

THE **MALES** OF THE PRICKLY DOGFISH ARE **SMALLER** THAN THE **FEMALES.** THE **MALES** ARE GENERALLY **TWO FEET LONG,** WHILE THE **FEMALES** CAN BE **TWO** AND A **HALF FEET LONG.**

ANGULAR ROUGHSHARK

Oxynotus centrina

Order Squaliformes (Dogfish Sharks)
Family Squalidae (Dogfish Sharks)

ANGULAR ROUGHSHARKS'
TOP TEETH ARE **SMALL**
AND **SPEAR-SHAPED.**
THE **BOTTOM TEETH**
ARE **SHAPED** MORE
LIKE A **BLADE.**

THE SKIN AROUND
THE **EYES** IS MUCH
ROUGHER THAN ON
THE REST OF THE **BODY.**

THE ANGULAR ROUGHSHARK
HAS **BIG, FLESHY LIPS.**

Length: 2 feet

WHERE THEY LIVE

THE ANGULAR ROUGHSHARK'S **BODY SHAPE** IS A LITTLE LESS **TRIANGULAR** THAN THE **PRICKLY DOGFISH.**

ANGULAR ROUGHSHARKS ARE GENERALLY **TWO FEET LONG,** BUT SOME CAN REACH **FIVE FEET** IN LENGTH.

THERE ARE **TWO DORSAL FINS,** FAR APART FROM EACH OTHER.

THE **ANGULAR ROUGHSHARK** IS FOUND AT DEPTHS BETWEEN **2** AND **20 FEET.**

THE ANGULAR ROUGHSHARK LIVES ON THE **BOTTOM** OF THE **SEAFLOOR,** SCOURING FOR **BRISTLE WORMS.**

WHAT THEY EAT

Small Bony Fish

Invertebrates
Worms and Snails

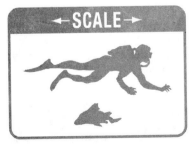

← SCALE →

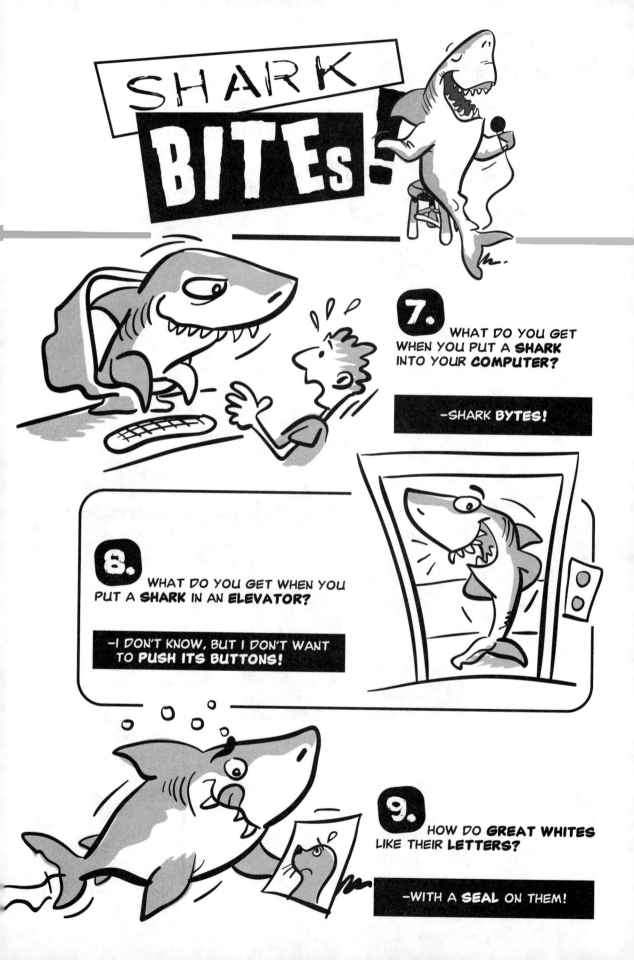

10. WHAT FISH **SURVIVED** THE **GREAT FLOOD?**

—NOAH'S **SHARK!**

11. AT WHAT **TIME** DOES A **SHARK** GO TO THE **DENTIST?**

—AT **TOOTH-HURTY!**

12. WHEN DID THE SHARK WIN THE **RACE?**

—WHEN IT CROSSED THE **FISHING LINE!**

SHARK Q&A

HOW MANY PEOPLE ARE KILLED BY SHARKS EVERY YEAR?

Sharks kill an average of ten people worldwide every year.

HOW MANY SHARKS ARE KILLED BY PEOPLE EVERY YEAR?

People kill an average of 100 million sharks every year.

SHARK Q&A

IS IT TRUE THAT THERE ARE **MORE SHARK ATTACKS** EVERY YEAR?

There are more shark attacks today than there were 100 years ago. This is because today more people are involved in water-related activities than before. But the average number of attacks have remained the same in recent years.

WHAT IS **TAGGING?**

Tagging is a method used by marine biologists to study sharks. After capturing a shark, scientists attach a tag to it. There are several kinds of tags. Some of them need to be attached to the shark's dorsal fin. Others are inserted into the shark's belly after a small operation. Then, the tagged shark is released into the water. The tag is a mini computer that collects information about water temperature and depths, where the shark goes, and how fast it swims.

AMAZING SHARK TEETH

THE **SHAPE** AND **SIZE** OF SHARKS' **TEETH** DEPENDS ON THEIR **FEEDING HABITS.** MOST SHARKS' TEETH ARE **EXTREMELY SHARP,** ALMOST **RAZOR-LIKE.** TEETH ARE USED TO **TEAR, CUT,** OR **CRUSH,** BUT NOT TO CHEW.

SHARKS HAVE **SEVERAL ROWS** OF TEETH AT **DIFFERENT STAGES** OF DEVELOPMENT. THE **MOST EXTERNAL ROW** IS THE ONE IN **USE,** THE **MOST INTERNAL ONE** IS THE **LEAST DEVELOPED.** SHARKS CAN HAVE UP TO **3,000 TEETH** IN THEIR **MOUTH** AND, THROUGHOUT THEIR **LIFE,** SHARKS CAN REPLACE **30,000 TEETH!**

WHEN A **TOOTH** IS **BROKEN** OR **FALLS OFF,** ANOTHER TOOTH TAKES ITS **PLACE.** SOME SHARKS, LIKE THE **COOKIE-CUTTER SHARK,** CAN REPLACE A **WHOLE ROW** OF TEETH AT ONE TIME. THEY ACTUALLY **SWALLOW** THEIR OWN TEETH, PROBABLY **RECYCLING** CALCIUM AND OTHER MINERALS.

MANY SHARKS HAVE **BIG, TRIANGULAR,** AND **SERRATED TEETH.** THESE SHARKS FEED ON **LARGE PREY** SUCH AS **SEA LIONS, SEALS,** AND **BIG BONY FISH.** THE **FORCE** SHARKS USE TO **BITE** IS SO **POWERFUL** IT CAN CUT THROUGH **BONES, TURTLE SHELLS,** AND, AS IT SOMETIMES HAPPENS, **SURF BOARDS!**

Great whites have serrated, triangular teeth that enable them to hunt for big prey.

SOME SHARKS HAVE
TEETH THAT ARE **THIN** AND
LONG. THESE TEETH ARE
PERFECT FOR CATCHING
SLIPPERY ANIMALS LIKE
OCTOPI, SQUID, AND **FISH.**

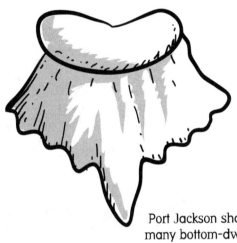

Lemon sharks use their bottom
teeth to impale their prey, and
the upper teeth to cut through it.

SHARKS THAT FEED
MOSTLY ON **CRABS** AND
CRUSTACEANS NEED
POWERFUL TEETH TO
CRUSH THE **SHELL** OF THEIR
PREY. THESE KIND OF TEETH
ARE GENERALLY LOCATED IN
THE **BACK** OF THE **MOUTH.**

AFTER HAVING CRUSHED
THE SHELL, MANY SHARKS
SWALLOW THE **WHOLE
PREY.** ONLY LATER ON, THEY
REGURGITATE THE **HARD
PARTS** THAT CANNOT
BE **DIGESTED.**

Port Jackson sharks, like
many bottom-dwelling sharks,
eat crustaceans and mollusks.

A **SHARK'S UPPER JAW** IS NOT **FUSED** TO ITS **SKULL,** AND IS
MOBILE LIKE THE **LOWER JAW.** WHEN SHARKS **CATCH** A **PREY,** THEIR
UPPER JAW **PROTRUDES** FROM THEIR **HEAD,** BITES THE **PREY,** AND
RETRACTS. IN THIS WAY, THE PREY IS **INESCAPABLY BROUGHT
INSIDE** THE **MOUTH.**

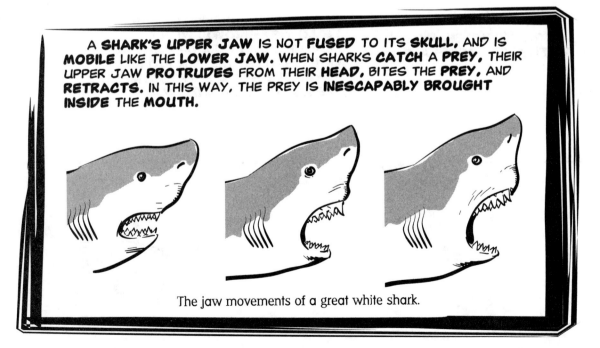

The jaw movements of a great white shark.

SWELL SHARK

Cephaloscyllium ventriosum

Order Carcharhiniformes (Ground Sharks)
Family Scyliorhinidae (Catsharks)

THE **SWELL SHARK** IS NAMED AFTER ITS **ABILITY** TO **SWELL UP** ITS BODY BY SWALLOWING **WATER.** EVEN THE LATIN NAME **VENTRIOSUM** REFERS TO THIS. THE WORD **VENTRIOSUM** MEANS "VENTER," OR "BELLY."

THE **EYES** ARE **OVAL** AND **BIG.**

THE **SWELL SHARK** HAS **NICTITATING MEMBRANES.**

THE SWELL SHARK'S **SKIN** IS **YELLOWISH-BROWN,** WITH A BEAUTIFUL **PATTERN** OF **DARK** AND **LIGHT SPOTS.** THE SKIN PATTERN MAKES THE SWELL SHARK **BLEND** INTO THE **ROCKY BACKGROUND.**

Length: 3.5 feet

←SCALE→

WHERE THEY LIVE

AN **ADULT** SWELL SHARK CAN BE **THREE** AND A **HALF** FEET LONG.

SWELL SHARKS **GATHER** IN **SMALL GROUPS** TO **REST TOGETHER.** SOMETIMES THEY **PILE UP** ON **TOP** OF **EACH OTHER.**

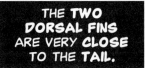

THE **TWO DORSAL FINS** ARE VERY **CLOSE** TO THE **TAIL.**

THE SWELL SHARK **LIVES** IN WATERS **10** TO **1,500 FEET DEEP.**

THE **SWELL SHARK** IS **NOCTURNAL,** MEANING IT **HUNTS** AT **NIGHT.**

SWELL SHARK

THE **PREDATORS** OF THE SWELL SHARK ARE **SHARKS, SEALS,** AND **SEA LIONS.**

WHEN A **SWELL SHARK** IS **CHASED** BY A PREDATOR, IT **HIDES** IN A **ROCK CREVICE** AND **SWALLOWS** A LOT OF **WATER.** WHEN ITS **BELLY SWELLS UP,** THE **SWELL SHARK** GETS **STUCK** IN THE **CREVICE,** AND ITS **PREDATOR CAN'T DRAG IT OUT.** AFTER THE **PREDATOR** LEAVES, THE SWELL SHARK **THROWS UP** THE **WATER** AND GETS OUT OF ITS HIDING PLACE.

ONCE OUT OF THE WATER, THE SWELL SHARK MAKES A **BARKING** SOUND BY **SWALLOWING AIR** AND **RELEASING** IT, AS MANY FISHERMEN CAN ATTEST. IT'S UNCLEAR IF THE SWELL SHARK **BARKS** WHEN **UNDERWATER.**

THIS SHARK CAN **DOUBLE** ITS **SIZE** SWALLOWING AIR OR **WATER!**

EACH **JAW** OF THE **SWELL SHARK** CAN HAVE **60 TEETH.**

TO **HUNT** ITS **PREY**, THE SWELL SHARK **LAYS STILL** ON THE **SEAFLOOR.** WHEN A **PREY** GOES BY **UNAWARE**, THE SWELL SHARK **SUCKS IT IN.**

WHAT THEY EAT

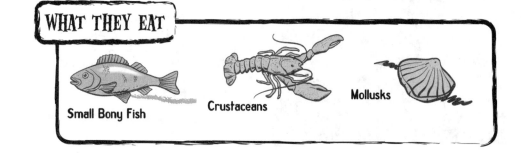

Small Bony Fish

Crustaceans

Mollusks

SWELL SHARK

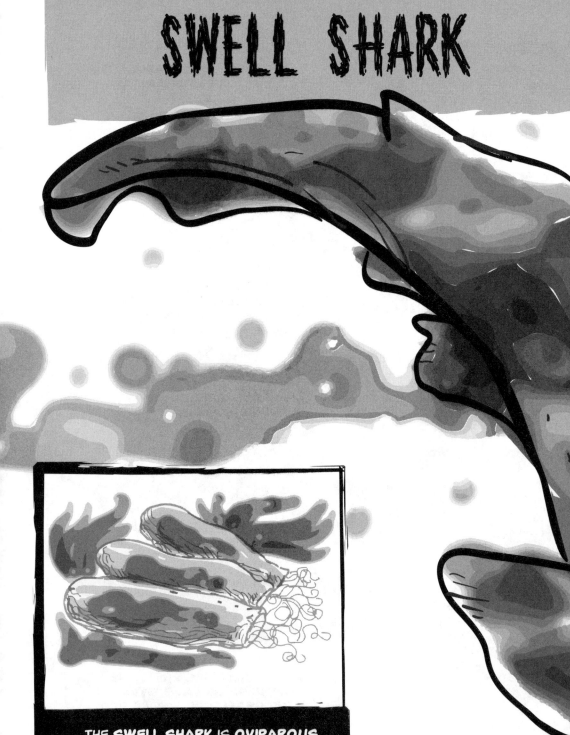

THE **SWELL SHARK** IS **OVIPAROUS.** THE FEMALE **DEPOSITS** ITS **EGGS,** HIDING THEM IN THE **UNDERSEA KELP,** A LARGE SEAWEED. THE **EGGS** LOOK LIKE **KELP,** AND **PREDATORS,** CONFUSING THEM FOR SEAWEED, **DON'T EAT** THEM.

SOMETIMES, THE SWELL SHARK TIES THE EGGS BY THE **TENDRILS** TO **ROCKS** AND **SEAWEED.**

WHEN THE **EGGS** ARE **DEPOSITED,** THEY ARE **LIGHT COLORED** AND **SOFT.** THEN, THEY BECOME **DARK BROWN** AND **GREEN,** AND **HARDEN.**

THE **EGGS** HAVE **CURLY TENDRILS** THAT LOOK LIKE THE **DRAWSTRING** OF A **PURSE.** THE SWELL SHARK'S EGGS ARE OFTEN CALLED **MERMAID'S PURSES.**

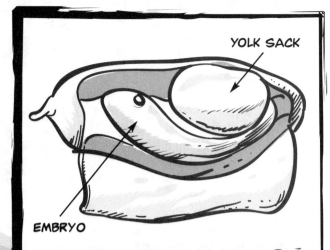

YOLK SACK

EMBRYO

INSIDE EACH **EGG** THERE'S AN **EMBRYO. THE YOLK** FEEDS THE **EMBRYO** WHILE IT GROWS.

IT TAKES **12 MONTHS** FOR THE **PUP** TO **HATCH.** THE PUP HAS SOME **HARD DENTICLES** ON **TOP** OF ITS **BACK.** WHEN IT'S TIME TO **HATCH,** THE PUP **CUTS** THE **EGG SHELL OPEN** WITH THEM.

PUPS ARE **5 INCHES** LONG.

CHAIN CATSHARK

Scyliorhinus retifer

Order Carcharhiniformes (Ground Sharks)
Family Scyliorhinidae (Catsharks)

THE **NAME** OF THIS SHARK REFERS TO THE **PATTERN** ON ITS **SKIN** THAT RESEMBLES A **CHAIN** OR **NET**. THE **COLOR** OF THE **BACK** IS **BROWN**, THE **BELLY** IS **PALE TAN**, WHILE THE **CHAIN-LIKE PATTERN** IS **DARK BROWN**, SOMETIMES **BLACK**.

THE **FIRST DORSAL FIN** IS ABOUT **TWICE** AS **BIG** AS THE **SECOND**. BOTH **DORSAL FINS** ARE POSITIONED **TOWARD** THE **TAIL**.

Length: 1.5 feet

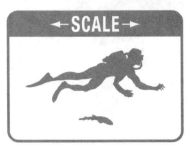

←**SCALE**→

WHERE THEY LIVE

MALES AND FEMALES ARE ABOUT THE SAME SIZE, BOTH MEASURING ABOUT ONE AND A HALF FEET IN LENGTH.

CHAIN CATSHARKS PREFER DEEP WATERS RANGING FROM 200 TO 1,500 FEET.

THE CHAIN CATSHARK SWALLOWS PEBBLES THAT IT CANNOT DIGEST. THE PEBBLES REMAIN IN ITS STOMACH AND GIVE THE CHAIN CATSHARK MORE WEIGHT, SO IT CAN STAY AT THE BOTTOM OF THE SEA.

WHAT THEY EAT

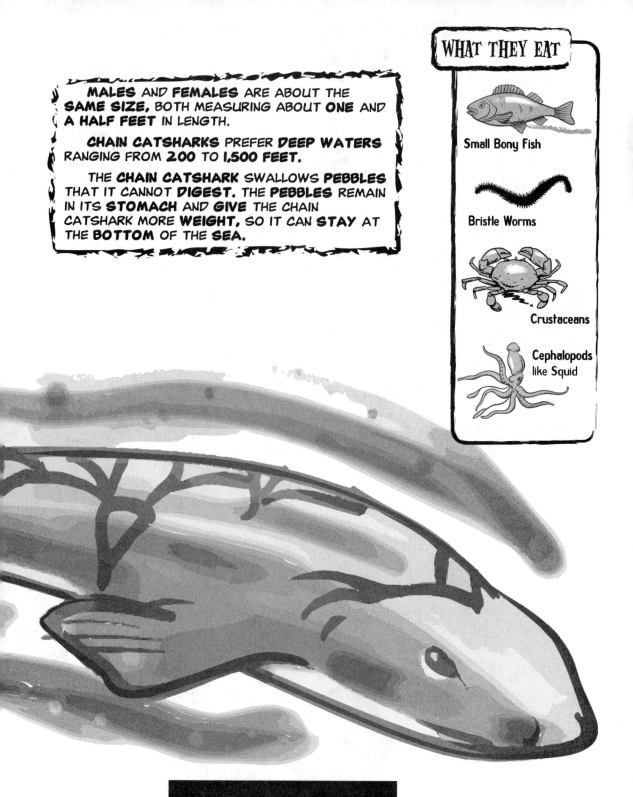

Small Bony Fish

Bristle Worms

Crustaceans

Cephalopods like Squid

THE PECTORAL FINS ARE ALMOST SQUARE. THE WIDTH AND THE LENGTH ARE APPROXIMATELY THE SAME.

DEEPWATER CATSHARK

Apristurus profundorum

Order Carcharhiniformes (Ground Sharks)
Family Scyliorhinidae (Catsharks)

UNLIKE THE SWELL SHARK, THE **DEEPWATER CATSHARK** HAS A **UNIFORM, BROWNISH-GREY SKIN COLOR.** THIS IS A **TYPICAL DIFFERENCE** BETWEEN **CATSHARKS** THAT LIVE **CLOSER** TO THE **SURFACE** AND THOSE THAT LIVE IN **DEEP WATERS.**

BOTH THE SWELL SHARK AND THE DEEPWATER CATSHARK **CAMOUFLAGE** THEMSELVES IN THE ENVIRONMENT IN WHICH THEY LIVE. THE SWELL SHARK HAS A **COLORFUL SKIN PATTERN,** SIMILAR TO THE **PATTERNS** AND **COLORS** OF **SHALLOW WATER SEA FLOORS.**

ON THE OTHER HAND, THE DEEPWATER CATSHARK HAS A **TONED-DOWN COLORATION.** THIS IS BECAUSE IT LIVES AT **DEPTHS** OF OVER **5,000 FEET,** WHERE THE **COLORS** OF THE **WATER** ARE MORE **UNIFORM** AND **DARK.**

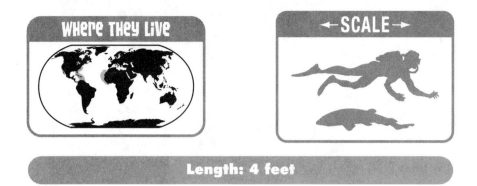

Length: 4 feet

THERE'S OVER **100 SPECIES** OF **CATSHARKS**, MORE THAN ANY OTHER **SHARK FAMILY!**

WHAT THEY EAT

Small Bony Fish

Bristle Worms

Crustaceans

Cephalopods like Squid

CORAL CATSHARK

Atelomycterus marmoratus

Order Carcharhiniformes (Ground Sharks)
Family Scyliorhinidae (Catsharks)

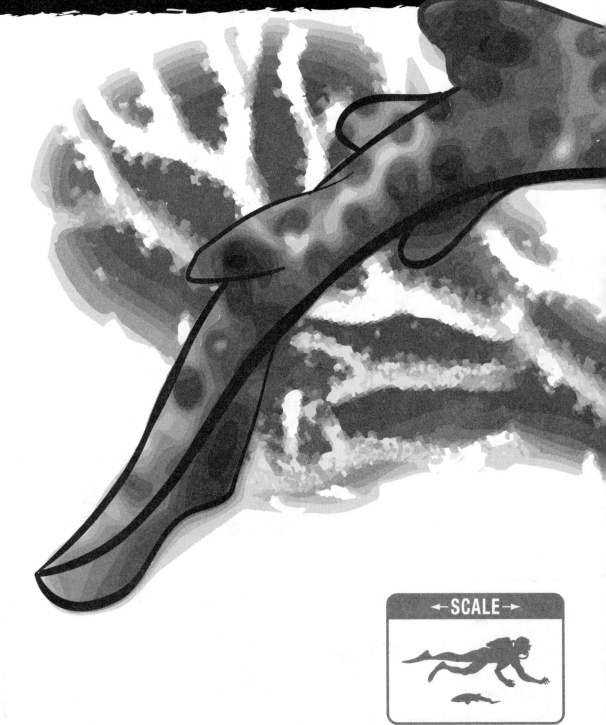

←SCALE→

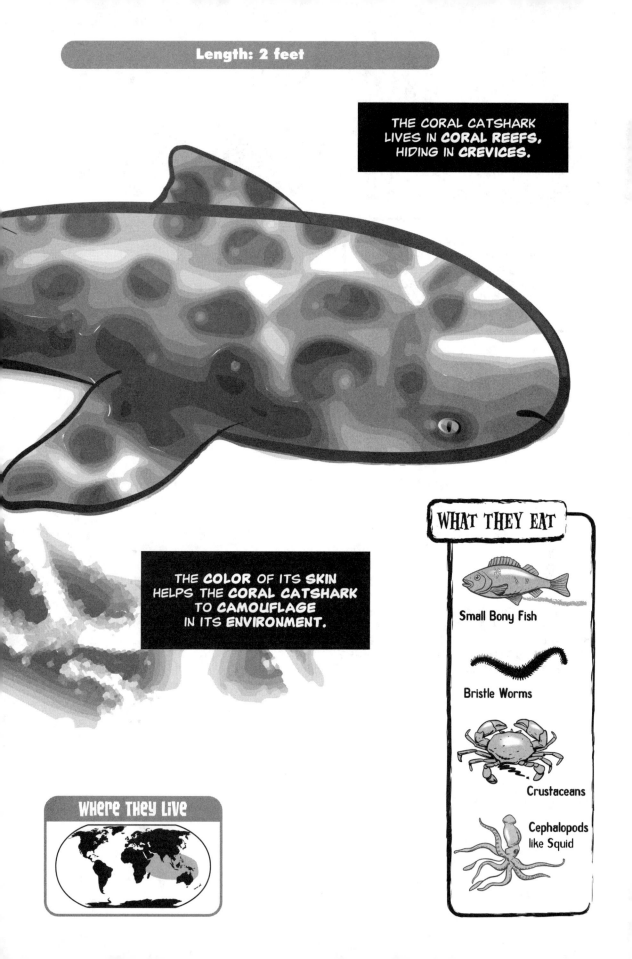

Length: 2 feet

THE CORAL CATSHARK LIVES IN **CORAL REEFS**, HIDING IN **CREVICES**.

THE **COLOR** OF ITS **SKIN** HELPS THE **CORAL CATSHARK** TO CAMOUFLAGE IN ITS **ENVIRONMENT**.

WHAT THEY EAT

Small Bony Fish

Bristle Worms

Crustaceans

Cephalopods like Squid

WHERE THEY LIVE

STRIPED (OR PAJAMA) CATSHARK

Poroderma africanum

Order Carcharhiniformes (Ground Sharks)
Family Scyliorhinidae (Catsharks)

THIS CATSHARK'S COMMON NAME, **PAJAMA CATSHARK**, WAS INSPIRED BY THE **PATTERN** ON ITS **SKIN**. THIS IS BECAUSE THE CLASSIC **CLOTH** USED TO MAKE **PAJAMAS** IS **STRIPED**.

THE **STRIPED CATSHARK** HAS **WHISKER-LIKE BARBELS** ON ITS **SNOUT**. WHEN THIS SHARK **SCOURS** THE **SEAFLOOR**, ITS **BARBELS** SENSE **PREY** THAT HIDE IN THE **SAND**.

Length: 3 feet

←SCALE→

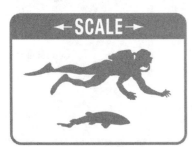

WHERE THEY LIVE

THIS CATSHARK IS **BROWNISH-GREY** WITH **DARK STRIPES.**

WHAT THEY EAT

Small Bony Fish

Cephalopods like Squid and Octopi

Clams

Worms

Crustaceans like Crabs and Shrimp

NURSEHOUND

Scyliorhinus stellaris

Order Carcharhiniformes (Ground Sharks)
Family Scyliorhinidae (Catsharks)

THE **NURSEHOUND** IS A **BOTTOM-DWELLER**. IT PREFERS **ROCKY SEAFLOORS**, OR ONES COVERED BY **SEAWEEDS**. NURSEHOUNDS ARE FOUND AT **SHALLOW DEPTHS** RANGING FROM **60** TO **200 FEET**.

THE BEAUTIFUL **PATTERN** ON THE **SKIN** OF THE NURSEHOUND IS VERY **SIMILAR** TO THAT OF A **LEOPARD**. THE **DIFFERENCE** IS THAT THE **NURSEHOUND'S** OVERALL **COLOR** IS **DARK BROWN** AND **GREY**. LEOPARDS ARE **YELLOW** WITH **DARK BROWN SPOTS**.

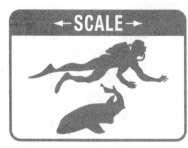

←SCALE→

WHERE THEY LIVE

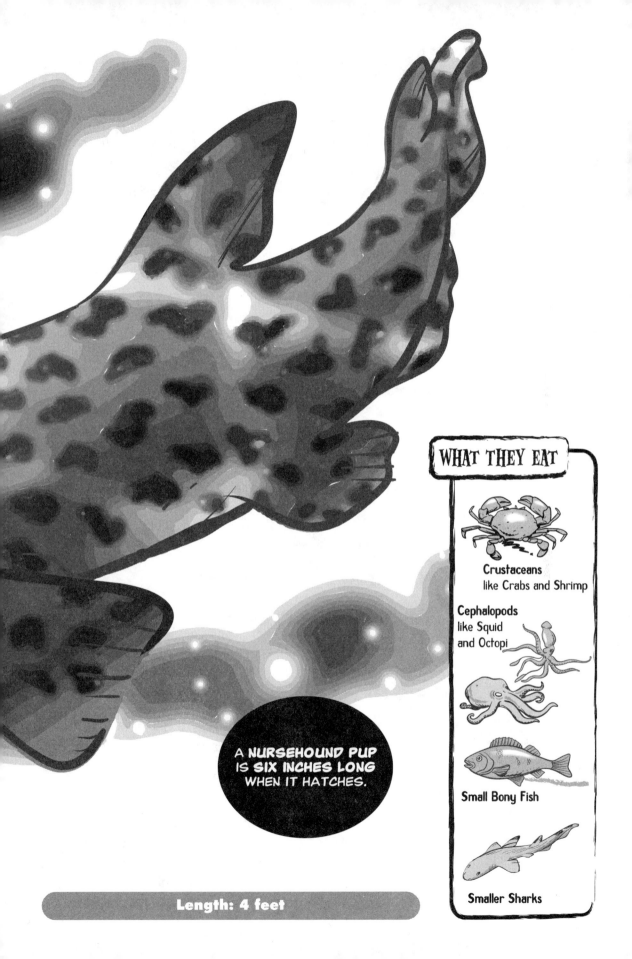

A NURSEHOUND PUP IS **SIX INCHES LONG** WHEN IT HATCHES.

WHAT THEY EAT

Crustaceans
like Crabs and Shrimp

Cephalopods
like Squid
and Octopi

Small Bony Fish

Smaller Sharks

Length: 4 feet

PYGMY RIBBONTAIL CATSHARK

Eridacnis radcliffei

Order Carcharhiniformes (Ground Sharks)
Family Proscyllidae (Finback Catsharks)

THE **PYGMY RIBBONTAIL CATSHARK** IS THE **SECOND SMALLEST** SHARK. **ADULT SHARKS** OF THIS SPECIES ARE ONLY BETWEEN **SIX** TO **NINE INCHES LONG.**

CATSHARKS' EYES ARE SIMILAR TO **CATS' EYES** IN **SHAPE** AND **COLOR.** ALSO, JUST LIKE CATS, SHARK EYES **GLOW** EERILY IN THE **DARK.** THESE **SIMILARITIES** INSPIRED THE COMMON NAME **CATSHARK.**

←SCALE→

WHERE THEY LIVE

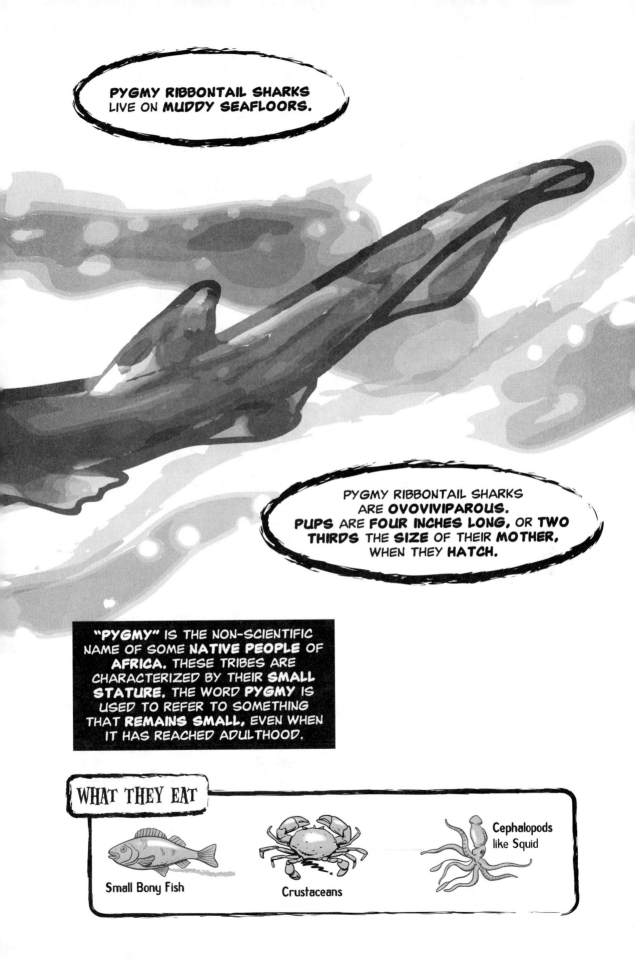

PYGMY RIBBONTAIL SHARKS LIVE ON **MUDDY SEAFLOORS.**

PYGMY RIBBONTAIL SHARKS ARE **OVOVIVIPAROUS.** PUPS ARE **FOUR INCHES LONG,** OR **TWO THIRDS** THE **SIZE** OF THEIR **MOTHER,** WHEN THEY **HATCH.**

"PYGMY" IS THE NON-SCIENTIFIC NAME OF SOME **NATIVE PEOPLE** OF **AFRICA.** THESE TRIBES ARE CHARACTERIZED BY THEIR **SMALL STATURE.** THE WORD **PYGMY** IS USED TO REFER TO SOMETHING THAT **REMAINS SMALL,** EVEN WHEN IT HAS REACHED ADULTHOOD.

WHAT THEY EAT

Small Bony Fish

Crustaceans

Cephalopods like Squid

FALSE CATSHARK

Pseudotriakis microdon

Order Carcharhiniformes (Ground Sharks)
Family Proscyllidae (Finback Catsharks)

THE LATIN NAME **MICRODON** MEANS **"SMALL TOOTH."** FALSE CATSHARK TEETH MIGHT BE SMALL, BUT THEY ARE **NUMEROUS!** EACH FALSE CATSHARK'S **JAW** CAN HAVE **200 ROWS** OF **TEETH!**

THE **MOUTH** IS **VERY LARGE.**

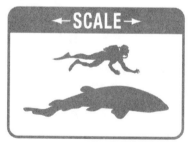

← SCALE →

THE **COLOR** IS **DARK BROWN.**

WHERE THEY LIVE

False catsharks are found in most oceans around the world.

FALSE CATSHARKS ARE **OVOVIVIPAROUS.** THE FEMALE **NOURISHES** ITS **EMBRYOS** BY **SECRETING** A WHITE SUBSTANCE CALLED **UTERINE MILK.** THE EMBRYOS ALSO **FEED** ON THE **UNHATCHED EGGS.**

Length: males, 9 feet; females, 10 feet

Shark Tales: Despite its presence in most oceans, the false catshark has shown up in US waters only twice. The first false catshark washed ashore in 1883 in Amagansett, Long Island, New York. The second one ran into a net in 1953 in Manasquam, New Jersey.

THE FALSE CATSHARK HAS A **VERY LONG DORSAL FIN.**

FALSE CATSHARKS LIVE IN WATERS **650** TO **5,000 FEET DEEP.**

WHAT THEY EAT

Small Bony Fish

Smaller Sharks

Batoids like Rays

Crustaceans

WHISKERY SHARK

Furgaleus macki

Order Carcharhiniformes (Ground Sharks)
Family Triakidae (Houndsharks)

THIS SHARK IS CALLED **WHISKERY** BECAUSE IT HAS **TWO THICK BARBELS,** OR **WHISKERS,** UNDER ITS **SNOUT.**

THEY HAVE A **WHITE BELLY,** WHILE THE REST OF THE **BODY** IS **COVERED** IN **LARGE, DARK BROWN** AND **GREY SPOTS.**

Length: 4 feet

WHERE THEY LIVE

← SCALE →

THE WHISKERY SHARK **LIVES** ON THE **SEAFLOOR** AT A **DEPTH** OF **700 FEET.**

THESE SHARKS PREFER **ROCKY SEA FLOORS** OR THOSE **COVERED** WITH **KELP** AND OTHER **SEAWEED.**

THE WHISKERY SHARK IS PERFECTLY **CAMOUFLAGED** TO **BLEND** INTO ITS **SURROUNDINGS** AND AVOID **PREDATORS.**

WHAT THEY EAT

Wiskery sharks mostly prey on Cephalopods.

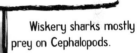

Cephalopods

Small Bony Fish

Crustaceans like Lobsters

Worms

Seaweed

THE WHISKERY SHARK IS **OVOVIVIPAROUS** AND HAS **LITTERS** OF ABOUT **20 PUPS.**

THE **FEMALES** GIVE BIRTH **EVERY OTHER YEAR.** THE **GESTATION** PERIOD LASTS **SEVEN MONTHS.**

PUPS ARE BORN BETWEEN **AUGUST** AND **OCTOBER.**

THE **PUPS** ARE ABOUT **NINE INCHES** LONG AT **BIRTH.**

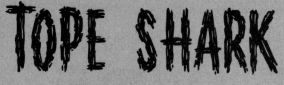

TOPE SHARK

Galeorhinus galeus

Order Carcharhiniformes (Ground Sharks)
Family Triakidae (Houndsharks)

SURPRISINGLY, THE SCIENTIFIC NAME **GALEORHINUS GALEUS** MEANS **"SHARK-NOSED SHARK"**! IT SOUNDS SILLY, DOESN'T IT?

THE TOPE SHARK HAS **NICTITATING MEMBRANES** TO **PROTECT** ITS **EYES**.

THE **SNOUT** IS VERY LONG.

← SCALE →

WHERE THEY LIVE

Length:
males, 6 feet;
females, 6.5 feet
Life span:
35 years

TOPE SHARKS FORM **GROUPS** TO **HUNT TOGETHER.** THE TOPE SHARKS ARE ABLE TO **HERD** A **SCHOOL** OF **FISH,** PUSHING IT AGAINST A **ROCK WALL** OR A **REEF.** WHEN THE SCHOOL HAS **NO PLACE TO GO** ANYMORE, TOPE SHARKS **PLUNGE INTO IT!**

A TOPE SHARK CAN **SWIM** A **DAILY AVERAGE** OF **30 MILES.**

ITS **BELLY** IS OF A VERY **LIGHT BLUE,** WHILE ITS **BACK** IS **DARK BLUE.**

THE TOPE SHARK LIVES NEAR THE BOTTOM OF THE OCEAN AT **DEPTHS** OF **1,500 FEET,** BUT THE **FEMALES** MOVE TO **SHALLOW WATERS** WHEN IT'S TIME TO **GIVE BIRTH.**

Shark Tales: This shark was first studied in 1757 by Carl Linnaeus, a Swedish scientist. Linnaeus came up with the idea of classifying animals and plants, and to give them two Latin names. His basic rules for naming animals and plants are still in use today.

SCHOOLS OF **TOPE SHARKS** MIGRATE TO THE **NORTHERN COLD WATERS** OF THE **ATLANTIC** AND **PACIFIC OCEANS** DURING THE **SUMMER.** IN THE **WINTER,** THEY MIGRATE BACK TO **WARMER WATERS.**

TOPE SHARK

THE **TOPE SHARK** IS **CAUGHT** FOR **FOOD** IN MANY COUNTRIES LIKE **AUSTRALIA, ARGENTINA, JAPAN,** AND **URUGUAY.**

THE **MEAT** OF THE **TOPE SHARK** IS VERY **RICH** IN **VITAMIN A.**

WHEN IT'S TIME TO **GIVE BIRTH,** TOPE SHARK **FEMALES** MEET IN VERY **SPECIFIC PLACES** EACH YEAR. THESE **PLACES** ARE CALLED **NURSERIES.** THE NURSERIES ARE IN AREAS WHERE THE **WATER** IS **WARM** AND NOT TOO **DEEP.**

EACH **TOPE SHARK FEMALE** CAN **GIVE BIRTH** TO 50 **PUPS.**

PUPS ARE **ONE FOOT** LONG AT **BIRTH.**

THE PUPS **REMAIN** IN THE NURSERIES FOR A **COUPLE OF YEARS.** THEN THEY **MOVE OUT** TO START THEIR **ADULT LIFE.**

 Shark Tales: An African delicacy called "biltong" is often made from the meat of tope sharks. It's prepared by adding some beef, vinegar, brown sugar, peppers, and spices to the meat of the tope shark. Then it's mixed and let marinate for 12 hours and hung to dry for 4 days. Enjoy!

WHAT THEY EAT

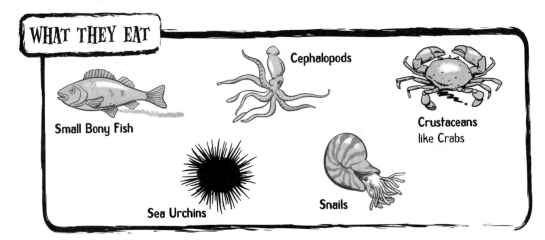

Cephalopods

Crustaceans
like Crabs

Small Bony Fish

Sea Urchins

Snails

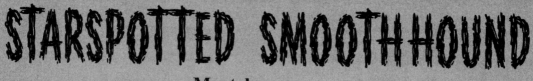

STARSPOTTED SMOOTHHOUND

Mustelus manazo

Order Carcharhiniformes (Ground Sharks)
Family Triakidae (Houndsharks)

THE **STARSPOTTED SMOOTHHOUND** WAS NAMED AFTER THE **BRIGHT WHITE SPOTS** ON ITS **DARK BROWN SKIN**. THEY LOOK LIKE **STARS** IN A **DARK SKY**.

THE **STARSPOTTED SMOOTHHOUND** PREFERS A **SANDY** OR **MUDDY SEAFLOOR**.

Length: 4 feet

THE LATIN WORD **MUSTELUS** MEANS "WEASEL."
THE GENUS NAME **MUSTELUS** BELONGS TO
SEVERAL SHARKS. ALL OF THEM HAVE A VERY
LONG SNOUT, LIKE THAT OF A **WEASEL.**

THEY **LIVE** AT A **DEPTH** OF 1,000 FEET.

←SCALE→

WHERE THEY LIVE

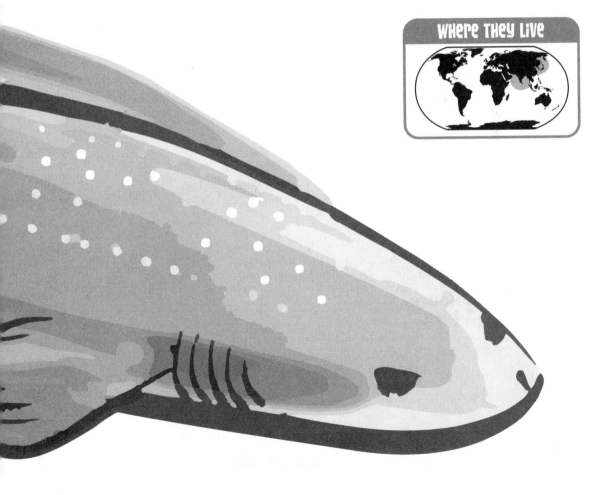

SNAGGLETOOTH SHARK

Hempristis elongatus

Order Carcharhiniformes (Ground Sharks)
Family Hemigaleidae (Weasel Sharks)

THE **SNAGGLETOOTH SHARK** IS THE **LONGEST SHARK** OF THIS **FAMILY**. IT CAN REACH **EIGHT FEET** IN LENGTH. ALL THE OTHER **WEASEL SHARKS** ARE MUCH SHORTER, OFTEN AROUND **FIVE FEET LONG**.

THEY HAVE **VERY ROUND EYES**.

THE SNAGGLETOOTH SHARK HAS **LONG LOWER TEETH**. THEY ARE SO LONG THAT THEY **STICK OUT** OF ITS **MOUTH**, EVEN WHEN IT IS **CLOSED**.

WHERE THEY LIVE

Length: 8 feet

THE **SNAGGLETOOTH SHARK** IS CONSIDERED A **DELICACY** IN INDIA.

SNAGGLETOOTH SHARKS LIVE AT **DEPTHS** OF **300 FEET**.

WHAT THEY EAT

Squid

Crabs

Small Bony Fish

Smaller Sharks

Batoids
like Rays

SILVERTIP SHARK

Carcharhinus albimarginatus

Order Carcharhiniformes (Ground Sharks)
Family Carcharhinidae (Requiem Sharks)

THE **SILVERTIP SHARK** IS **BLUISH-GREY**, FADING TO **WHITE** ON ITS **BELLY**.

THE LATIN WORDS **CARCHARHINUS ALBIMARGINATUS** MEAN **"SHARP-NOSED [SHARK] WITH WHITE TIPS."** THIS SHARK HAS **WHITE BLOTCHES** AT THE **TIPS** OF ITS **FINS**.

WHERE THEY LIVE

SCALE

SILVERTIP SHARKS ARE SHY AND SWIM AWAY IF THEY FEEL THREATENED. BUT THEY CAN GET VERY AGGRESSIVE IN THE PRESENCE OF FOOD OR BAIT.

SOMETIMES A SILVERTIP SHARK SWIMS ALONGSIDE A SCHOOL OF HUNTING SHARKS OF A DIFFERENT SPECIES. WHEN THE TIME IS RIGHT, THE SILVERTIP SHARK RUSHES INTO THE SCHOOL AND STEALS THEIR PREY.

WHAT THEY EAT

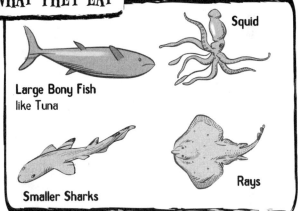

Squid

Large Bony Fish like Tuna

Smaller Sharks

Rays

THE SILVERTIP SHARKS LIVE IN WATERS OFF OF LITTLE ISLANDS AND SHORE REEFS. THIS SHARK IS COMMONLY FOUND AT DEPTHS OF 2,500 FEET.

THE SILVERTIP SHARK IS VIVIPAROUS AND ITS LITTER CAN SPAWN EIGHT PUPS. A SILVERTIP SHARK PUP IS TWO FEET LONG. THE PUPS LIVE CLOSER TO THE COASTS, AVOIDING PREDATORS.

Length: 9 feet

SPINNER SHARK

Carcharhinus brevipinna

Order Carcharhiniformes (Ground Sharks)
Family Carcharhinidae (Requiem Sharks)

THE **SPINNER SHARK** OWES ITS **NAME** TO ITS WAY OF **HUNTING.** WHEN A SCHOOL OF PREY **SWIMS ABOVE** IT, THE SPINNER SHARK **SPINS UPWARD, SNAPPING** AT **FISH** WITH ITS **MOUTH** AS IT GOES. SOMETIMES IT **CANNOT STOP** ITSELF AND ENDS UP **JUMPING OUT** OF THE **WATER!**

THE SPINNER SHARK HAS A VERY **POINTY SNOUT.**

ITS **TEETH** ARE **NEEDLE-LIKE** TO **BETTER GRASP** ITS **PREY.**

THE **SKIN COLOR** IS **DARK GREY** TO **WHITE.** THERE'S A **WHITE LINE** ALONG ITS **SIDES.**

←SCALE→

WHERE THEY LIVE

THE FEMALE'S **GESTATION PERIOD** LASTS FOR MORE THAN **ONE YEAR**. THE SPINNER SHARK IS **VIVIPAROUS** AND GIVES BIRTH TO **TEN PUPS**.

PUPS REMAIN **CLOSE** TO THE **SHORE** UNTIL THEY ARE **BIG ENOUGH** TO SURVIVE IN **DEEPER WATERS**.

IT'S FOUND AT DEPTHS OF **100 FEET**.

THE SPINNER SHARK HAS **BLACK TIPS** ON ITS **PECTORAL, SECOND DORSAL**, AND **ANAL FINS**.

Length: 6.5 feet
Weight: 125 lbs.

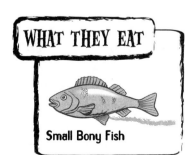

WHAT THEY EAT

Small Bony Fish

SILKY SHARK

Carcharhinus falciformis

Order Carcharhiniformes (Ground Sharks)
Family Carcharhinidae (Requiem Sharks)

THE COMMON NAME **SILKY SHARK** REFLECTS THE **SMOOTHNESS** OF THIS **SHARK'S SKIN**. THE SKIN IS SMOOTH BECAUSE THE **DENTICLES** ARE **VERY SMALL** AND **NUMEROUS**.

THE SILKY SHARK LIVES AT **DEPTHS** OF **50 FEET** TO **1,500 FEET**.

THE SILKY SHARK HAS A **LONG FREE REAR TIP** ON ITS **TWO DORSAL FINS**. THE **SECOND ONE** IS **PARTICULARLY LONG**. A **FREE REAR TIP** IS THE **POINTY PART** OF THE **FIN** THAT IS **NOT ATTACHED** TO THE **BODY**.

WHERE THEY LIVE

← SCALE →

THE SILKY SHARK IS **VIVIPAROUS** AND GIVES BIRTH TO ABOUT **EIGHT PUPS.** THE PUPS ARE **BORN** IN **SPRING.** AT BIRTH A PUP IS ABOUT **TWO** AND **A HALF FEET LONG.**

THIS SHARK HAS **VERY LARGE EYES.**

SILKY SHARK'S **UPPER TEETH** ARE **TRIANGULAR** AND **SERRATED,** WHILE THE **BOTTOM ONES** ARE MUCH **THINNER** AND **SMOOTHER.** THE BOTTOM TEETH ARE USED TO **HOLD** ON TO A **PREY.** THE UPPER TEETH **CUT** THROUGH IT.

THE **COLOR** OF THE **SKIN** IS **DARK GREY** ON TOP, GRADUALLY BECOMING **LIGHT TAN** UNDERNEATH.

Length: males, 10 feet; females are slightly bigger
Life span: less than 25 years

SILKY SHARK

WHEN **ANIMALS** FEEL **THREATENED**, THEY EITHER **RUN AWAY**, OR THEY **WARN**
THEIR **ATTACKER** THAT THEY ARE **GETTING ANGRY**. FOR EXAMPLE, A **DOG**
SHOWS ITS **TEETH** AND **GROWLS**. SILKY SHARKS, TOO, HAVE A WAY OF SHOWING
WHEN THEY FEEL HARASSED. THEY **ARCH** THEIR **BACKS**, **RAISE** THEIR **HEADS**,
AND **LOWER** THEIR **TAILS** RIGHT **BEFORE ATTACKING**. THIS **DISPLAY** HAS BEEN
NOTICED IN SILKY SHARKS AND IN **OTHER SPECIES** LIKE THE **GREAT WHITES**.

Shark Tales: Silky sharks often swim along tuna schools for a quick bite.

WHAT THEY EAT

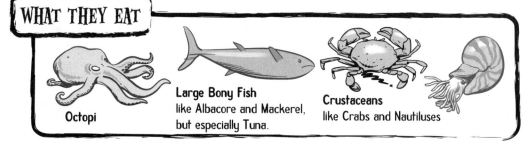

Octopi

Large Bony Fish
like Albacore and Mackerel, but especially Tuna.

Crustaceans
like Crabs and Nautiluses

BULL SHARK

Carcharhinus leucas

Order Carcharhiniformes (Ground Sharks)
Family Carcharhinidae (Requiem Sharks)

THE **BULL SHARK** IS VERY **AGGRESSIVE** AND ITS **BODY** IS **STOUT**, LIKE A **BULL!**

THE **COLOR** OF THE **SKIN** IS **DARK GREY**, GRADUALLY FADING TO **WHITE** UNDERNEATH. **PUPS** HAVE **DARKER FIN TIPS**.

THE **SECOND DORSAL FIN** IS MUCH **SMALLER** THAN THE **FIRST**.

WHERE THEY LIVE

←SCALE→

Length: males, 7 feet; females, 8 feet.
Weight: males, 200 lbs.; females, 280 lbs.
Life span: males, 13 years; females, 15 years.

ITS **EYES** ARE
VERY SMALL.

THE BULL SHARK HAS A
SHORT AND **ROUNDED**
SNOUT. THE **WIDTH** OF
THE **SNOUT** IS **BIGGER**
THAN ITS **LENGTH.**

THE **UPPER TEETH** ARE
TRIANGULAR AND
SERRATED, THE **LOWER**
TEETH ARE **THINNER** AND
LESS SERRATED THAN THE
UPPER ONES.

BULL SHARK FEMALES CONGREGATE IN
NURSERIES. NURSERIES ARE PLACES IN **SHALLOW**
AND **WARM WATERS** WHERE BULL SHARKS **GIVE**
BIRTH. BULL SHARK NURSERIES ARE FOUND GENERALLY
NEAR **RIVER ESTUARIES,** IN **BRACKISH WATERS.**
THESE **WATERS** ARE A **MIX** OF **SEA** AND **FRESH**
WATERS, AND THE **SALT CONTENT** IS LOWER THAN
THE OCEAN.

THE BULL SHARK IS **VIVIPAROUS** AND HAS A
GESTATION PERIOD OF **TEN MONTHS.** THE AVERAGE
LITTER SPAWNS **13 PUPS.** PUPS ARE BORN IN **LATE**
SPRING AND **EARLY SUMMER.** THEY ARE OVER **TWO**
FEET LONG AT **BIRTH.**

BULL SHARKS HAVE **NO PREDATORS,** BUT BULL
SHARK **PUPS** ARE SOMETIMES **PREYED ON** BY BULL
SHARK **ADULTS.**

BULL SHARK

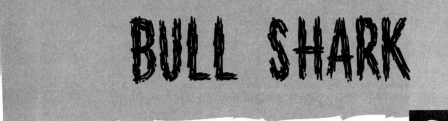

BULL SHARKS ARE ONE OF THE **FEW SHARKS** THAT **TOLERATE FRESH WATERS.** THEY CAN SWIM IN **ESTUARIES** AND UP **RIVERS** FOR **MILES.**

BULL SHARKS ARE FOUND IN THE **AMAZON RIVER,** IN PERU, **2,500 MILES** AWAY FROM THE **ATLANTIC OCEAN!**

BULL SHARKS ARE ALSO FOUND IN THE **MISSISSIPPI RIVER** IN **ILLINOIS,** AFTER **SWIMMING** UPSTREAM FOR NEARLY **3,000 MILES** FROM THE **GULF OF MEXICO.**

BULL SHARKS ARE FOUND IN **LAKE NICARAGUA.** AT FIRST, THE **SHARKS** OF **LAKE NICARAGUA** WERE THOUGHT TO BE A **DIFFERENT SPECIES.**

IT TURNED OUT THAT **BULL SHARKS** CAN SWIM FROM THE **CARIBBEAN SEA** UP THE **SAN JUAN RIVER, JUMPING** UP THE **RAPIDS** LIKE A **SALMON,** AND **REACH** THE **LAKE!**

BULL SHARKS ARE FOUND IN THE **ZAMBESI RIVER** IN **AFRICA**, AND IN THE **GANGES RIVER** IN **INDIA**.

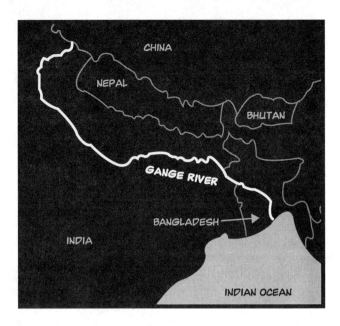

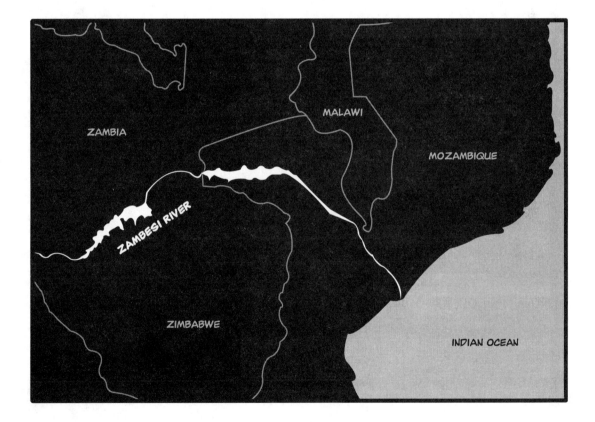

BULL SHARKS SWIM **CLOSE** TO THE **COASTS**, AT **DEPTHS** OF **LESS** THAN **100 FEET** TO **500 FEET**. THEY ARE OFTEN FOUND IN **MURKY WATERS**.

BULL SHARK

WHAT THEY EAT

Bony Fish

Other Sharks
(sometimes their own kind)

Batoids
like Rays

Crabs and Shrimp

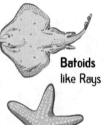

Echinoderms
like Starfish, Sea Urchins,
and Sea Cucumbers

Octopi

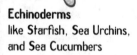

Mollusks

Seabirds

Marine Mammals
like Dolphins

Sea Snails

Sea Turtles

Garbage

BULL SHARKS **APPEAR** TO BE **SLOW SWIMMERS**, BUT BECOME VERY **ACTIVE** AND **AGGRESSIVE** IN THE PRESENCE OF **FOOD**. SO FAR, THEY HAVE BEEN **RESPONSIBLE** FOR **70 KNOWN UNPROVOKED ATTACKS** ON **PEOPLE**, 16 OF WHICH WERE **FATAL**.

THE BULL SHARK WANDERS IN **SHALLOW** AND **WARM WATERS**, THE **SAME PLACES** IN WHICH **PEOPLE** ENJOY TO **SWIM**.

THE **NUMBER** OF **ATTACKS** IS **PROBABLY HIGHER**. THE BULL SHARK ISN'T AS **EASILY RECOGNIZABLE** AS OTHER **DANGEROUS SHARKS** BECAUSE OF ITS **BLAND SKIN COLOR**.

Shark Tales: Bull sharks eat anything they can sink their teeth in. Some of the things that were found in the stomach of this shark are dogs, hippos, crocodiles, and garbage.

BLACKTIP SHARK

Carcharhinus limbatus

Order Carcharhiniformes (Ground Sharks)
Family Carcharhinidae (Requiem Sharks)

THE COMMON NAME **BLACKTIP SHARK** REFERS TO THE **BLACK COLORATION** ON THE **TIP** OF THE **FINS**.

THE **BLACKTIP SHARK** OFTEN SWIMS NEAR **RIVER ESTUARIES**, BUT NEVER WANDERS INTO THE **RIVERS**. UNLIKE THE **BULL SHARK**, THE BLACKTIP SHARK CANNOT SURVIVE IN **FRESHWATER**.

THE **FIRST DORSAL FIN** IS POSITIONED **BEHIND** THE **PECTORAL FINS**.

THE **ONLY FIN** THAT IS NOT **TIPPED BLACK** IS THE **ANAL FIN**. THE TIPS ARE **DARKER** IN **YOUNG SHARKS** AND BECOME **LIGHTER** IN **ADULTS**.

WHERE THEY LIVE

THE **COLOR** OF THE **SKIN** IS **DARK BLUISH-GREY**, SOMETIMES **BROWN**, FADING TO **WHITE** UNDERNEATH. THERE IS A **WHITE LINE** ON **BOTH SIDES**, FROM ABOVE THE **PECTORAL FINS** TO THE **TAIL**.

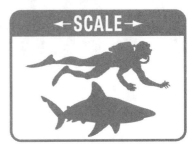

← SCALE →

THE BLACKTIP SHARK IS FOUND IN WATERS UP TO **100 FEET DEEP**.

BLACKTIP SHARKS ARE **VERY ACTIVE** AND OFTEN **AGGRESSIVE**.

THERE ARE NO **SPIRACLES** ON ITS HEAD NOR **BARBELS** ON ITS **SNOUT**. THESE CHARACTERISTICS ARE TYPICAL OF **FAST-MOVING SHARKS**.

THE **BODY** IS **STOUT** AND THE **SNOUT** IS **POINTY**.

THE **LOWER TEETH** ARE **MORE SERRATED** THAN THE **UPPER ONES**.

Length: 5 feet
Weight: 40 lbs.
Life span: 15 years

Shark Tales: Blacktip sharks have been responsible for about 30 recorded non-fatal attacks on people. They are known to harass divers, bumping into them with their snout. But they are generally shy and prefer to swim away if they feel threatened.

BLACKTIP SHARK

THE **BLACKTIP SHARK** IS **VIVIPAROUS**. LITTERS HAVE UP TO **10 PUPS**, AND THE **GESTATION** PERIOD LASTS **12 MONTHS**.

THE **BLACKTIP SHARK FEMALES** CREATE **NURSERIES** IN **WARM** AND **SHALLOW WATERS**. THEIR **PUPS** REMAIN THERE FOR A **FEW YEARS** BEFORE VENTURING INTO **DEEPER WATERS**. THIS WAY, PUPS AVOID **PREDATORS** UNTIL THEY ARE **OLD ENOUGH** TO **DEFEND THEMSELVES**.

A **BLACKTIP SHARK PUP** IS ABOUT **ONE FOOT** LONG AT BIRTH.

Blacktip shark pups at birth.

BLACKTIP SHARKS ATTACK **SCHOOLS** OF FISH BY **SWIMMING VERTICALLY** THROUGH THEM. WHILE SWIMMING VERTICALLY, BLACKTIP SHARKS **SPIN** THEIR **BODY** AND **SNAP** THE **FISH**. SOMETIMES THEY **CAN'T STOP** THEMSELVES BEFORE **REACHING** THE **SURFACE** AND ARE SEEN **JUMPING** OUT OF THE **WATER**.

BLACKTIP SHARKS CAN BE CAUGHT IN A **FEEDING FRENZY**. IN THE PRESENCE OF **FOOD**, BLACKTIP SHARKS BECOME SO **AGGRESSIVE**, THEY **ATTACK** AND **INJURE** EACH OTHER. A BLACKTIP SHARK **BADLY INJURED** IN A FEEDING FRENZY MIGHT END UP BEING **EATEN** BY ITS **OWN KIND**!

A blacktip shark swimming through a school of fish.

WHAT THEY EAT

Small Bony Fish

Smaller Sharks

Batoids
like Rays and Stingrays

Cephalopods
like Squid

Crustaceans

OCEANIC WHITETIP SHARK

Carcharhinus longimanus

Order Carcharhiniformes (Ground Sharks)
Family Carcharhinidae (Requiem Sharks)

AS THEIR **COMMON NAME** SUGGESTS, **OCEANIC WHITETIP SHARKS** HAVE **WHITE SPOTS**. ITS **FIRST DORSAL, CAUDAL,** AND **BOTH PECTORAL FINS** ALL HAVE **WHITE TIPS**.

SURPRISINGLY, THE **PUPS** OF THIS SPECIES HAVE **DARK SPOTS** ON THE **TIP** OF THEIR **FINS**.

THE **TOP** OF THE **FIRST DORSAL FIN** IS **VERY ROUND**, JUST LIKE THE **TWO PECTORAL FINS**.

BOTH THE **FIRST** AND **SECOND DORSAL FINS** HAVE **LONG FREE REAR TIPS**.

THE LATIN NAME **LONGIMANUS** MEANS **"LONG HANDS"** AND REFERS TO THIS SHARK'S **LONG PECTORAL FINS**.

THE **SKIN COLOR** IS **GREY** OR **DARK BROWN**, FADING TO **WHITE**.

← SCALE →

WHERE THEY LIVE

Length: 10 feet
Life span: 20 years

THE **OCEANIC WHITETIP SHARK** IS GENERALLY FOUND AT **500 FEET** OF **DEPTH**. SOMETIMES IT SWIMS **CLOSE** TO THE **SHORES** OF **OCEANIC ISLANDS**.

THEY LIKE **WATERS** THAT ARE AROUND **70°** **FAHRENHEIT** AND **MIGRATE** TO **WARMER WATERS** IF THE TEMPERATURE **DROPS**.

THE OCEANIC WHITETIP SHARK HAS A **STOUT BODY** AND A **BLUNT SNOUT**.

THE **UPPER TEETH** ARE **TRIANGULAR** AND **SERRATED**, WHILE THE **LOWER** ONES ARE **THIN**. THE **UPPER TEETH** ARE USED TO **BITE**, WHILE THE **BOTTOM ONES** HOLD THE **PREY**.

THE **EYES** ARE **SMALL**.

THE **DENTICLES** ARE **FLAT** AND THE **SKIN** IS **SMOOTH**.

FEMALES GIVE **BIRTH** IN THE **SUMMER** AND **PUPS** ARE UP TO 15 PER **LITTER**.

AN OCEANIC WHITETIP SHARK PUP CAN BE **2 FEET LONG** AT **BIRTH**.

SOMETIMES PUPS HAVE A **LARGE, SADDLE-SHAPED, DARK SPOT** BETWEEN THE **FIRST** AND THE **SECOND DORSAL FINS**.

OCEANIC WHITETIP SHARK

DESPITE ITS PREFERENCE FOR **DEEP WATERS,** WHERE **PEOPLE** ARE UNLIKELY TO **SWIM,** THIS SHARK IS CONSIDERED **EXTREMELY DANGEROUS.** THE **OCEANIC WHITETIP SHARK** WAS **RESPONSIBLE** FOR MANY **FATALITIES** DURING **WORLD WAR II.** WHEN **WAR SHIPS** AND **PLANES** WERE **HIT,** THE **SURVIVORS** WERE OFTEN **ATTACKED** BY THIS SHARK.

OCEANIC WHITETIP SHARKS ARE KNOWN TO **CIRCLE SCUBA DIVERS,** PERSISTENTLY **INVESTIGATING** THEIR **ACTIVITIES.** THE SHARK IS **NOT DISCOURAGED** EVEN WHEN THE DIVER **PUNCHES** IT IN AN ATTEMPT TO **CHASE** IT **AWAY.**

Shark Tales: Remora, and sometimes turtles, follow the oceanic whitetip shark.

THE OCEANIC WHITETIP SHARK HAS A VERY **SIMPLE HUNTING TECHNIQUE.** IT **SWIMS THROUGH** A **SCHOOL** OF **TUNA** WITH ITS **MOUTH** WIDE **OPEN.** WITHOUT MUCH EFFORT, IT **SWALLOWS** ALL THE **TUNA** THAT **ACCIDENTALLY** GET INTO ITS **MOUTH.**

OCEANIC WHITETIP SHARKS OFTEN **FOLLOW** GROUPS OF **SHORTFIN PILOT WHALES** TO **STEAL** THEIR **FOOD.**

IT'S GENERALLY A **VERY SLOW-SWIMMING** SHARK, BUT BECOMES **EXTREMELY FAST, AGGRESSIVE,** AND **BOLD** IN THE **PRESENCE** OF **FOOD.**

WHAT THEY EAT

Small Bony Fish

Batoids like Rays

Sea Turtles

Crustaceans

Marine Mammals like Dolphins

Seabirds

Cephalopods

Gastropods

Garbage and Carcasses of Dead Animals

BLACKTIP REEF SHARK

Carcharhinus melanopterus

Order Carcharhiniformes (Ground Sharks)
Family Carcharhinidae (Requiem Sharks)

THE **BLACKTIP REEF SHARK** HAS **BLACK SPOTS** ON THE **TIPS** OF **ALL** ITS **FINS.** THE TWO **MOST STRIKING** SPOTS ARE LOCATED ON THE TIP OF THE **DORSAL FIN** AND ON THE **LOWER LOBE** OF THE **CAUDAL FIN.**

THERE'S A **WHITE STRIPE** UNDER THE **BLACK SPOT** ON THE **DORSAL FIN** THAT MAKES THE **TIP** EVEN MORE **PROMINENT.**

THE **EYES** ARE **OVAL-SHAPED.**

THE **SNOUT** IS **BLUNT** AND **ROUNDED.**

BLACKTIP REEF SHARK'S **TEETH** ARE **NARROW** AND **SERRATED** TO CATCH SMALL, **SQUIRMY FISH** AND **SQUID.**

Length: 6 feet

←SCALE→

THERE ARE UP TO **FOUR PUPS** PER **LITTER.**

WHERE THEY LIVE

Recently, blacktip reef sharks have moved into the Southern part of the Mediterranean Sea from the Red Sea, through the Suez Channel.

THE BLACKTIP REEF SHARK BECOMES **AGGRESSIVE** IN THE **PRESENCE** OF **SPEARFISHING DIVERS.**

THE BLACKTIP REEF SHARK'S **FAVORITE HABITAT** IS **CORAL REEFS.** IT'S ALSO FOUND IN **MANGROVE AREAS** DURING **HIGH TIDE.**

ALTHOUGH THE BLACKTIP REEF SHARK HAS NEVER BEEN INVOLVED IN **FATALITIES,** IT HAS BEEN REPORTED **BITING** THE **FEET** OF **PEOPLE** WANDERING IN **KNEE-HIGH WATERS.**

THE **SECOND DORSAL FIN** HAS A **SHORT FREE REAR TIP.**

THE **SKIN COLOR** IS **YELLOWISH-BROWN,** FADING TO **WHITE** ON THE **BELLY.**

THE BLACKTIP REEF SHARK SWIMS IN **SHALLOW WATERS** UP TO A **DEPTH** OF LESS THAN **300 FEET.**

WHAT THEY EAT

Small Bony Fish

Crustaceans

Cephalopods

CARIBBEAN REEF SHARK

Carcharhinus perezi

Order Carcharhiniformes (Ground Sharks)
Family Carcharhinidae (Requiem Sharks)

AS THE COMMON NAME SUGGESTS, *CARIBBEAN REEF SHARKS* LIVE IN THE **CORAL REEFS** OF THE CARIBBEAN WATERS.

THE **SECOND DORSAL FIN** HAS A **SHORT FREE REAR TIP.**

←SCALE→

WHERE THEY LIVE

Length: 8 feet

THE CARIBBEAN REEF SHARK IS **VIVIPAROUS.**

A CARIBBEAN REEF SHARK'S **LITTER** CAN SPAWN **FOUR** TO **SIX PUPS.**

THESE SHARKS SPEND **MANY HOURS** EVERY DAY **MOTIONLESS** AT THE **BOTTOM** OF THE **SEA** OR IN **CAVES.** THEY DON'T VENTURE INTO **WATERS** MORE THAN **100 FEET DEEP.**

THE **SNOUT** IS **BLUNT** AND **ROUNDED.**

WHAT THEY EAT

Small Bony Fish

Crustaceans like Lobsters

Octopi

TIGER SHARK

Galeocerdo cuvier

Order Carcharhiniformes (Ground Sharks)
Family Carcharhinidae (Requiem Sharks)

TIGER SHARKS HAVE **SPIRACLES** ON THEIR HEADS. SPIRACLES ARE **OPENINGS** NEAR THE **EYES** THAT **AID** THE **BREATHING PROCESS.** TIGER SHARKS MAINLY BREATHE WITH THEIR **MOUTH** AND **GILLS.**

THE **EYES** ARE **VERY LARGE.**

THE **SNOUT** IS **ROUNDED** AND **BLUNT.**

THE **SKIN COLOR** IS **DARK BLUISH-GREY** ON TOP, FADING TO **WHITE.** THE MOST PROMINENT **SKIN FEATURES** ARE THE **DARK SPOTS** AND **STRIPES** ON THE BACK. THEY INSPIRED THE NAME **TIGER SHARK.**

WHERE THEY LIVE

Tiger sharks migrate to the warmer parts of the oceans during the winter.

← SCALE →

Length: 15 feet
Weight: 1,300 lbs.

THE TIGER SHARK SPENDS THE **DAY** IN **DEEP WATERS** AND COMES **CLOSER** TO **SHORE** AT NIGHT.

THE **TIGER SHARK** IS ONE OF THE **BIGGEST SHARKS**. IT CAN BE UP TO **15 FEET** LONG AND WEIGH UP TO **1,300 POUNDS**.

TIGER SHARKS LIVE IN THE **MUDDY WATERS** OF **RIVER ESTUARIES** AND IN THE **SHALLOW WATERS** OF **OCEANIC ISLANDS**.

THE SKIN'S **DARK MARKS** TEND TO **FADE** WITH **AGE**.

THE BODY IS **STOUT** FROM THE **SNOUT** TO THE **PELVIC FINS**, THEN IT **BECOMES SLENDER** AND **LONG**.

THE **TIGER SHARK** IS ONE OF THE **MOST COMMON** SHARKS IN THE WORLD.

BOTH THE **UPPER** AND **LOWER** TEETH ARE **TRIANGULAR** AND **SERRATED**. THEY ARE **CURVED BACKWARD** AND HAVE A **DEEP NOTCH** ON ONE

Shark Tales: Tiger sharks can make trans-oceanic migrations travelling 50 miles a day, on average.

TIGER SHARK

TIGER SHARKS APPEAR TO BE **SLUGGISH**, BUT BECOME **AGGRESSIVE** IN THE **PRESENCE** OF **FOOD**.

TIGER SHARKS FIND THEIR PREY USING THEIR **EXTREMELY SOPHISTICATED SENSES**. ONCE DISCOVERING A POSSIBLE PREY, THE TIGER SHARK **CIRCLES** IT, **NUDGES** AT IT, AND THEN **MOVES IN** FOR THE **KILL**.

TIGER SHARKS ARE **EXTREMELY DANGEROUS**, SECOND ONLY TO THE **GREAT WHITE**. TIGER SHARKS HAVE BEEN RESPONSIBLE FOR **MANY ATTACKS** ON **PEOPLE**, SOME OF THEM **FATAL**. DESPITE THIS, TIGER SHARKS **DON'T HUNT PEOPLE**, AS HUMANS ARE NOT PART OF THEIR **NATURAL DIET**.

THE TIGER SHARK IS THE ONLY **OVOVIVIPAROUS** SHARK IN THE **REQUIEM SHARK FAMILY.** THIS MEANS THAT THE **EGGS** HATCH **INSIDE** THE **MOTHER'S BODY,** AND THE MOTHER GIVES BIRTH TO **LIVE YOUNG.**

DURING THE **GESTATION PERIOD,** TIGER SHARK **FEMALES** PRODUCE A **WHITE SUBSTANCE** CALLED **UTERINE MILK** TO FEED THEIR **EMBRYOS.**

PUPS ARE **BORN** DURING THE **SPRING** AND **EARLY SUMMER.**

PUPS ARE OVER **2 FEET LONG** AT **BIRTH.** THEY ARE BORN AFTER A **GESTATION PERIOD** OF ABOUT **15 MONTHS.**

A **LITTER** CAN **PRODUCE** AS MANY AS **80 PUPS!**

Shark Tales: Often tiger sharks swallow items that cannot be digested. To rid themselves of these items, tiger sharks vomit them by flipping their stomachs out of their mouth.

WHAT THEY EAT

Sea Turtles

Small Bony Fish

Other Sharks

Batoids

Crustaceans

Seabirds

Dolphins and Small Whales

Garbage and Carcasses

Octopi

Reptiles

Tiger sharks are definitely not picky eaters. They would gulp down anything that is remotely considered food. Besides carrion, which may include carcasses of dogs and deer, tiger sharks eat garbage. Some of the items that have been found in their stomachs include plastic bottles, canned food, coal, coats, and burlap bags.

LEMON SHARK

Negaprion brevirostris

Order Carcharhiniformes (Ground Sharks)
Family Carcharhinidae (Requiem Sharks)

THE LATIN NAME **NEGAPRION** MEANS **"WITHOUT SAW"** AND REFERS TO THE **EDGES** OF THE **LEMON SHARK'S TEETH.** THEY ARE IN FACT **SERRATED** ONLY AT THEIR **BASE.**

THE LATIN NAME **BREVIROSTRIS** MEANS **"SHORT-NOSED"** AND REFERS TO THE LEMON SHARK'S **BLUNT SNOUT.**

THE LEMON SHARK'S **SKIN** IS **YELLOWISH-GREY** ON TOP, FADING INTO A **WHITISH-YELLOW** ON ITS BELLY. THIS **COLOR** INSPIRED THIS SHARK'S **COMMON NAME.**

THE **BODY** IS **STOUT.**

Length: 10 feet

WHERE THEY LIVE

GROUPS OF LEMON SHARKS ARE FOUND IN **SHALLOW WATERS,** GENERALLY AT **NIGHT.** DURING THE **DAY,** THESE SHARKS WANDER INTO **WATERS** UP TO **300 FEET.**

LEMON SHARKS LIVE IN **CORAL REEFS, MANGROVES,** AND **RIVER ESTUARIES.**

LEMON SHARKS ARE **VIVIPAROUS**. THIS MEANS THAT THE **EMBRYOS** ARE **CONNECTED** TO THEIR MOTHER'S **PLACENTA** THROUGH AN **UMBILICAL CORD**. IT ALSO MEANS THAT THE **MOTHER** GIVES BIRTH TO **LIVE YOUNG**, AS OPPOSED TO LAYING EGGS.

LEMON SHARKS GIVE BIRTH DURING THE **SUMMER**, AFTER A GESTATION PERIOD OF **12 MONTHS**. FOR THIS REASON, FEMALES CAN ONLY GIVE BIRTH **EVERY OTHER YEAR**.

THE **PUPS** ARE **BORN** IN **NURSERIES**. NURSERIES ARE PLACES IN **SHALLOW** AND **WARM WATERS** WHERE LEMON SHARK FEMALES **CONGREGATE** TO GIVE **BIRTH**.

A **LITTER** CAN PRODUCE **5** TO **18** PUPS, **2 FEET** LONG EACH.

PUPS REMAIN IN THE **NURSERIES** FOR **SEVERAL YEARS** BECAUSE THEY **GROW** VERY **SLOWLY**. PUPS **DON'T WANDER** INTO OPEN **SEAS** BECAUSE THEY MIGHT BE EATEN BY **BIGGER SHARKS**.

← SCALE →

WHAT THEY EAT

Small Bony Fish

Crustaceans
like Crabs and Crayfish

Batoids
like Stingrays and
Eagle Rays

Seabirds

Other Sharks
(sometimes other
Lemon sharks!)

BLUE SHARK

Prionace glauca

Order Carcharhiniformes (Ground Sharks)
Family Carcharhinidae (Requiem Sharks)

THE LATIN NAME **PRIONACE**, WHICH MEANS **"POINTY SAW,"** REFERS TO THE BLUE SHARK'S **SHARP, SERRATED TEETH.**

THE LATIN NAME **GLAUCA** MEANS **"BLUE"** AND WAS INSPIRED BY THE **SKIN COLOR** OF THIS SHARK. THE BLUE FADES INTO **WHITE** ON THE **BELLY.**

THE **PECTORAL FINS** ARE VERY **LONG** AND **POINTY.**

WHERE THEY LIVE

Blue sharks live in warm and temperate seas and oceans. They sporadically wander into colder waters.

← SCALE →

THESE **SHARKS** SWIM RARELY NEAR THE **SHORE** AND LIVE BETWEEN THE **SURFACE** TO **DEPTHS** OF 1,200 FEET.

AN **ADULT BLUE SHARK** CAN MEASURE ABOUT **10 FEET** IN LENGTH. SOME PEOPLE REPORTED HAVING SEEN SOME **BLUE SHARKS** THAT WERE OVER **20 FEET LONG!**

BLUE SHARKS' **UPPER TEETH** ARE **CURVED, SERRATED TRIANGLES.** THE **BOTTOM TEETH** ARE MUCH **THINNER** AND **WITHOUT SERRATION.**

THE **SNOUT** IS **LONG** AND **POINTY.**

Length: 10 feet

THE **NUMBER** OF **PUPS** IN A LITTER IS **PROPORTIONAL** TO THE **SIZE** OF THE **MOTHER.** THE **BIGGER** THE **BLUE SHARK** FEMALE, THE **MORE NUMEROUS** ITS **LITTER** IS.

THE **GESTATION PERIOD** IS ABOUT **10 MONTHS LONG** AND A **LITTER** CAN SPAWN **130 PUPS!**

BLUE SHARK

THE **BLUE SHARK** IS ONE THE **MOST COMMON SHARKS.** IT'S ALSO CONSIDERED ONE OF THE **MOST BEAUTIFUL,** BECAUSE OF ITS **GRACEFUL SHAPE, PRETTY COLOR,** AND **BIG EYES.**

SCHOOLS OF BLUE SHARKS PERIODICALLY **MIGRATE** FOR **EXTENDED DISTANCES.**

A **TAGGED BLUE SHARK** SWAM FROM **NEW ZEALAND** TO **CHILE,** COVERING A **STAGGERING DISTANCE** OF ALMOST **800 MILES!**

Shark Tales: Some requiem sharks, like the blue shark, remain in a sleep-like state of frozen lethargy if turned upside down. This motionless mood is called "tonic immobility." A shark in a state of tonic immobility doesn't move, doesn't feel pain, and seems to be unaware of its surroundings. The duration of tonic immobility is extremely variable, but scientists use this trick by flipping sharks on their backs for routine check-ups. Strangely enough, chickens are also subject to tonic immobility if picked up and laid carefully on their backs.

THE **PREDATORS** OF THE **BLUE SHARK** ARE **GREAT WHITES** AND THE **SHORTFIN MAKOS.**

THE BLUE SHARK'S **HUNTING TECHNIQUE** INVOLVES **CIRCLING** ITS **PREY** AND THEN CLOSING IN FOR AN **EXPLORATORY BITE.** IF THE SHARK LIKES THE **TASTE,** IT GOES IN FOR THE **KILL.**

BLUE SHARKS HAVE BEEN RESPONSIBLE FOR MANY **ATTACKS** ON **PEOPLE,** SEVERAL OF WHICH WERE **FATAL.**

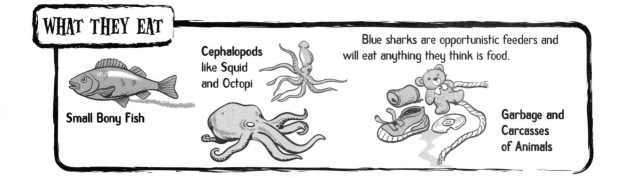

WHAT THEY EAT

Small Bony Fish

Cephalopods like Squid and Octopi

Blue sharks are opportunistic feeders and will eat anything they think is food.

Garbage and Carcasses of Animals

WHITETIP REEF SHARK

Triaenodon obesus

Order Carcharhiniformes (Ground Sharks)
Family Carcharhinidae (Requiem Sharks)

WHITETIP REEF SHARKS HAVE
BRIGHT WHITE SPOTS ON THEIR
FIRST DORSAL FIN AND TAIL.
OFTEN, BUT NOT ALWAYS, THE
TIP OF THE SECOND DORSAL
FIN IS WHITE, TOO.

←SCALE→

WHERE THEY LIVE

This shark doesn't live in the Atlantic ocean, but many of its fossils have been found there. The fossils are over five million years old. This proves that during the Miocene period, whitetip reef sharks inhabited the Atlantic.

Length: 5 feet
Life span: over 20 years

WHITETIP REEF SHARKS ARE **CURIOUS**, BUT **NOT AGGRESSIVE** TOWARD DIVERS. WHEN THEY FEEL THREATENED, THEY'D RATHER **SWIM AWAY** THAN **ATTACK**. WHITETIP REEF SHARKS MIGHT BECOME **AGGRESSIVE** IF THE DIVER HAS **SPEARED FISH**. EVEN SO, THIS IS NOT CONSIDERED A **DANGEROUS SHARK**.

WHITETIP REEF SHARKS ARE **NOCTURNAL** AND **HUNT** DURING THE **NIGHT**.

THE **SHALLOW WATER** OF THE **CORAL REEFS** IS THE **PREFERRED ENVIRONMENT** OF THE WHITETIP REEF SHARK.

THIS SHARK'S **EYES** ARE **OVAL** AND **PROTECTED** BY **RIDGES**.

ITS **COLOR** IS **DARK BROWN**, FADING TO **LIGHT TAN**.

THE **HEAD** IS **FLATTENED** AND THE **SNOUT** IS **BLUNT**.

WHITETIP REEF SHARK

WHITETIP REEF SHARKS ARE **VIVIPAROUS** AND CAN HAVE UP TO **FOUR PUPS.**

THE **GESTATION** PERIOD LASTS FOR ABOUT **FIVE MONTHS.**

EACH PUP CAN BE UP TO **ONE** AND **A HALF FEET LONG** AT BIRTH.

 Shark Tales: In Hawaii, the whitetip reef shark is called an "aumakua." People believe this shark to be the reincarnation of one of their ancestors and a protector of the family. Other sharks, like the blacktip reef shark and the hammerhead shark, share this honor. For this reason, Hawaiians would never hunt them.

DURING THE **DAY,** GROUPS OF **WHITETIP REEF SHARKS** ARE OFTEN FOUND **RESTING** ON THE **OCEAN FLOOR** IN **CAVES.** SOMETIMES THERE ARE SO MANY OF THEM THAT THEY **PILE UP** ON **EACH OTHER.** EACH GROUP SEEMS TO PREFER A **SPECIFIC CAVE,** WHERE THEY RETURN **EVERY DAY.**

DURING THE **NIGHT,** GROUPS OF **WHITETIP REEF SHARKS** GO ON A **HUNT.** THEY CHASE THEIR PREY RELENTLESSLY. OFTEN THEY **JAM** THEIR **BODIES** INTO **SMALL CREVICES,** THROUGH THE **SHARP EDGES** OF THE **CORAL REEF,** WHERE THEIR **PREY** IS TRYING TO HIDE. FORTUNATELY, THE WHITETIP REEF SHARK'S **SKIN** IS PARTICULARLY **TOUGH.**

THEY ARE **EXTREMELY TENACIOUS** SHARKS THAT DON'T GIVE UP **CHASING** THEIR PREY. THEIR CHASE OFTEN **BRINGS** HAVOC AND **DESTRUCTION** TO THE **CORAL REEF.**

WHAT THEY EAT

Cephalopods like Octopi

Crustaceans
like Crabs and Lobsters

Small Bony Fish

SCALLOPED HAMMERHEAD

Sphyrna lewini

Order Carcharhiniformes (Ground Sharks)
Family Sphyrnidae (Hammerhead Sharks)

THE **HAMMERHEAD SHARK'S** MOST **PROMINENT FEATURE** IS ITS **HAMMER-SHAPED HEAD.** THE ANCIENT GREEK WORD **SPHYRNA** MEANS "HAMMER." THIS **SHARK'S** HEAD HAS **INDENTATIONS,** HENCE THE NAME **SCALLOPED.**

THE **ANAL FIN** HAS A MARKED **NOTCH** AND A **LONG FREE REAR TIP.**

WHeRe THeY LiVe

THE **HEAD** CAN MEASURE **4 FEET**, OR UP TO **30%** OF THE **LENGTH** OF THE **BODY**. THE **SIDES** OF THE **HEAD** ARE **ARCHED** AND THE **REAR CORNERS** POINT **BACKWARD**.

SOMETIMES, SCALLOPED HAMMERHEADS ARE FOUND IN **BRACKISH WATERS**, NEAR **RIVER ESTUARIES**.

THE **MOUTH** IS IN A **SHAPE** OF AN **UPSIDE DOWN "U."**

SOME **SCALLOPED HAMMERHEADS** MAKE **YEARLY MIGRATIONS** TO **COLDER** WATERS DURING THE **SUMMER**. OTHERS REMAIN IN THE **SAME LOCATION** ALL **YEAR-ROUND**.

Length: 11 feet
Weight: 350 lbs.
Life span: over 30 years

← SCALE →

THE **SKIN COLOR** IS **GREENISH-GREY** ON TOP, FADING TO **WHITE** ON THE SHARK'S **BELLY**.

SCALLOPED HAMMERHEADS LIVE NEAR THE **COASTS** AT **DEPTHS** OF **1,000 FEET**.

THE **SCALLOPED HAMMERHEAD** IS THE **MOST COMMON** OF THE **HAMMERHEAD SHARKS**.

SCALLOPED HAMMERHEAD

BIG SCHOOLS OF MOSTLY SCALLOPED HAMMERHEAD **FEMALES** CONGREGATE IN THE **PACIFIC OCEAN** OFF THE COASTS OF **CALIFORNIA** AND **MEXICO.** THESE SHARKS PREFER SWIMMING AROUND **UNDERWATER MOUNTAINS** OR NEAR **ISLANDS.** IN THESE PLACES, SCALLOPED HAMMERHEADS OFTEN DISPLAY A **STRANGE BEHAVIOR.** THEY **NUDGE** INTO EACH OTHER WITH THEIR SNOUTS, **SHAKE** THEIR **HEADS,** AND SWIM **VERTICALLY** IN **SPIRALS.** ALTHOUGH THIS BEHAVIOR HAS BEEN NOTED ON **MANY OCCASIONS,** THE **MEANING** OF IT REMAINS A **MYSTERY.**

WHILE **YOUNG HAMMERHEADS** FORM **BIG SCHOOLS,** OLDER **HAMMERHEADS** MIGHT LIVE **ALONE** OR IN **SMALLER GROUPS.**

Shark Tales: Scalloped hammerheads routinely visit cleaning stations. A cleaning station is a place where small fish, called wrasses, live. Hammerheads let wrasses pick up and eat the parasites that live on their skin and inside their mouths.

SCALLOPED HAMMERHEADS ARE **NOCTURNAL**. THEY STAY **CLOSER** TO THE **SHORES** DURING THE **DAY**, AND WANDER **FURTHER** INTO THE **OCEAN** AT **NIGHT** TO HUNT.

SCALLOPED HAMMERHEADS EAT **STINGRAYS** AND ARE **IMMUNE** TO THE **POISON** OF THE **STINGER**. STINGRAY STINGERS HAVE BEEN FOUND **EMBEDDED** IN SCALLOPED HAMMERHEAD **MOUTHS** AND **STOMACHS**.

BOTH **DORSAL FINS** HAVE **FREE REAR TIPS**. THE **FREE REAR TIP** ON THE **SECOND DORSAL FIN** IS **LONGER**.

THE **TIPS** OF THE **PECTORAL FINS** OFTEN ARE **DARKER** THAN THE **REST** OF THE **BODY**. THIS CHARACTERISTIC IS MORE PRONOUNCED IN **YOUNGER SCALLOPED HAMMERHEADS**.

WHAT THEY EAT

Small Bony Fish

Octopi

Crustaceans like Crabs, Lobsters, and Shrimp

Batoids like Rays and Stingrays

Other Sharks

SCALLOPED HAMMERHEADS ARE **VIVIPAROUS** AND CAN SPAWN BETWEEN **15** AND **30 PUPS**.

THE **GESTATION** PERIOD LASTS **10 MONTHS** AND THE **PUPS** ARE **BORN** IN **SHALLOW-WATER NURSERIES**.

THE **LENGTH** OF AN AVERAGE **PUP** IS ABOUT **ONE** AND **A HALF FEET** AT **BIRTH**.

GREAT HAMMERHEAD

Sphyrna mokarran

Order Carcharhiniformes (Ground Sharks)
Family Sphyrnidae (Hammerhead Sharks)

THE **GREAT HAMMERHEAD** **SKIN COLOR** IS **GREY** ON TOP, FADING TO **WHITE.**

GREAT HAMMERHEADS HAVE A **NOTCH** IN THE **MIDDLE** OF THEIR **HEAD.** THE HEAD OF THE GREAT HAMMERHEAD **JUVENILES** IS **CURVED,** WHILE THE **HEAD** OF **OLDER** HAMMERHEADS IS **STRAIGHT.**

THE **GREAT HAMMERHEAD** IS THE **BIGGEST SHARK** OF THE **HAMMERHEAD FAMILY.**

GREAT HAMMERHEADS **MIGRATE** TO **COOLER WATERS** DURING THE **SUMMER.**

THEY LIVE NEAR THE **COASTS** AT **DEPTHS** OF **1,000 FEET.**

HAMMERHEADS ARE **VIVIPAROUS.** A **LITTER** CAN YIELD UP TO **40 PUPS.** PUPS ARE **2 FEET** LONG AT **BIRTH.**

THE **SCIENTIFIC NAME** FOR THE HAMMER-SHAPED HEAD IS **CEPHALOFOIL.**

THE **TEETH** OF THE **GREAT HAMMERHEAD** ARE **TRIANGULAR, SLIM,** AND **SERRATED.** THE **TEETH** OF THE **SCALLOPED HAMMERHEAD** ARE **SIMILAR** IN SHAPE, BUT THEY ARE **NOT SERRATED.**

GREAT HAMMERHEADS **SWING** THEIR **HEAD** FROM **SIDE** TO **SIDE** TO HAVE A **BETTER VIEW** OF THEIR **SURROUNDINGS** WHILE THEY **SWIM.**

WHERE THEY LIVE

←SCALE→

GREAT HAMMERHEAD

IT HAS BEEN NOTED THAT
WHEN **FOOD** IS PRESENT,
HAMMERHEADS ARE THE
FIRST SHARKS TO APPEAR.

THE HAMMERHEADS' FAVORITE
PREY, **STINGRAYS** AND
ANGELSHARKS, SPEND MOST OF
THEIR TIME **BURIED** IN THE **SAND.**
THEY ARE **IMPOSSIBLE** TO **SEE** TO
THE NAKED EYE. TO FIND THEM,
HAMMERHEADS **SWING** THEIR **HEAD**
FROM **SIDE** TO **SIDE,** LIKE A
METAL-DETECTOR. IN THIS WAY,
THEIR **AMPULLAE** OF **LORENZINI** CAN
EFFICIENTLY **SENSE** THE **PRESENCE** OF
THE BURIED PREY'S **ELECTRIC FIELD.** ALL
SHARKS HAVE **AMPULLAE,** BUT BECAUSE
THE **HAMMERHEAD'S HEAD** IS **WIDER,** THE
AMPULLAE ARE ABLE TO **COVER** MORE
GROUND. THIS MAKES THE HAMMERHEAD
MORE **SUCCESSFUL** AT **HUNTING.**

ONCE THE HAMMERHEAD **SENSES** ITS
BURIED PREY, IT **DIGS IT OUT** WITH
ITS **HEAD.**

ANOTHER REASON FOR THE
HAMMER-SHAPED HEAD IS THAT
THE **NOSTRILS** ARE **FARTHER APART**
THAN IN OTHER SHARKS. THIS GIVES
THE HAMMERHEADS A **WIDER RANGE**
IN THEIR **SMELLING.** IT ENABLES
THEM TO **PERCEIVE** MORE **ODORS**
AT ONE TIME AND HAVE A **BETTER**
IDEA OF **WHERE** THE ODORS
COME FROM.

HAMMERHEADS ARE CONSIDERED **DANGEROUS** BECAUSE OF THEIR **SIZE** AND BECAUSE THEY HAVE BEEN **RESPONSIBLE** FOR A **FEW NON-FATAL ATTACKS** ON **PEOPLE.** BUT GENERALLY HAMMERHEADS **DON'T ATTACK** DIVERS.

Length: 13 feet
Weight: 500 lbs.
Life span: 30 years

WHAT THEY EAT

Small Bony Fish

Cephalopods
like Squid
and Octopi

Crustaceans
like Crabs, Lobsters,
and Shrimp

Batoids
like Stingrays,
Butterfly rays,
and Guitarfish

Sharks
Great
hammerheads
sometimes eat
each other.

wEirD
SHARK
FACTOIDS

Sharks aren't the ferocious eating machines portrayed in movies. Actually, sharks can go for quite some time without eating, simply recycling the nutrient oils found in their livers. The record for the longest fast belongs to a captive swell shark, which spent almost two months without eating!

The Belle Isle Aquarium in Detroit reported that one spotted bamboo shark had given birth to two pups. This was an amazing event because the shark hadn't had any contact with males of its species for the previous seven years! So far, scientists have not been able to explain the event.

The reported shark attacks on humans show that sharks attack more men than women. This could be due to the fact that, around the world, more men are involved in water-related activities than women.

Every year, squid congregate in huge schools to mate. Their mating lasts for only a few hours. Right after depositing their precious fertilized eggs, the squid die.

Such numerous congregations are a great attraction for all sorts of predators, including the opportunistic blue sharks.

Blue sharks have been observed feasting on the squid, simply swimming through the school with their mouths wide open. There are so many squid, and so little time, that blue sharks regurgitate partially digested squid to feast on fresh ones!

To protect themselves against attacks, researchers dive in shark-infested waters wearing a metal suit. This suit is made of interlocking steel links and looks very much like the chain mail medieval soldiers used to wear. The metal suit is flexible enough for the diver to move around, but it cannot be penetrated by the sharpest of shark's teeth.

ARE YOU KEEPING ME OUT, OR YOU IN?

For those who want to dive with sharks, but don't care to wear a metal suit, a sturdy cage is the answer! There are many tours available where tourists are locked into a metal cage and dropped in the ocean. From the safety of the cage, tourists can have close encounters even with the most feared sharks, the great whites.

BUOYANCY

Bony Fish

Buoyancy is the ability to remain afloat. In order not to sink, bony fish have a swim bladder. A swim bladder is a pouch filled with air positioned in the fish's belly.

Air is lighter than water and tends to go upward, balancing the weight of the fish and keeping it from sinking.

The swim bladder enables the bony fish to float in the water at the proper depth. The movements of the fins and body propel the fish forward.

Some species of bony fish are able to extract oxygen from their blood and use it to fill their swim bladders. Other species simply swallow some air.

Sharks

A sand
tiger shark.

S... ... ... In order not to sink, sharks rely
... ...led liver. The oil in the liver is lighter than
... ...es the shark a
certain amount of buoyancy.

But a shark needs more than a large liver in order not to sink. For this reason, sharks have to continuously swim.

Some sharks have figured out how to use air to their advantage. Sand tiger sharks go to the surface and swallow air, filling their stomach with it. Then, they fart out the excess, until they reach the proper depth in the water. In this way, sand tiger sharks don't have to constantly swim and can actually remain motionless in mid-water.

Bottom-dweller sharks don't need to be buoyant. "Negative buoyancy" is the tendency to sink due to the body weight and lack of a swim bladder. Angelsharks use their negative buoyancy to remain on the ocean floor, hiding in the sand to ambush their prey.

An angelshark
hiding under
the sand.

SQUALENE

The liver is positioned in the belly of the shark.

The oil that fills a shark's liver is composed mainly of a fatty substance called squalene. Squalene is also found in small quantities in olive oil, wheat germ oil, and rice bran oil.

Squalene is very rich in vitamins A and D, and it's used in skin care products.

80% of the liver of most sharks consists of oil. In some sharks the percentage is higher, 90%. A shark's liver is so big it makes up to 30% of the shark's total weight.

Some sharks can survive without eating for long periods of time, even two months, by recycling the oil in their livers.

A bluntnosed sixgill shark.

"SHARK JUSTICE!"

A Fish Tale Like None You've Ever Heard!

Thomas Briggs

Captain Lieutenant Hugh Wylie

Kit

FRILLED SHARK

Chlamydoselachus anguineus

Order Hexanchiformes (Sixgill and Sevengill Sharks)
Family Hexanchidae (Sixgill and Sevengill Sharks)

THE **LATIN** NAME **CHLAMYDOSELACHUS ANGUINEUS** MEANS "**EEL-LIKE CAPED SHARK.**" THE COMMON NAME **FRILLED SHARK** REFERS TO THE **FRILLS** ON ITS **GILLS.**

THERE ARE **SIX GILL SLITS** ON EACH SIDE OF THE HEAD. THE FIRST GILL **ENCIRCLES** THE **HEAD.**

THE **MOUTH** IS **TERMINAL.** THIS MEANS THAT THE MOUTH IS IN **FRONT** OF THE SNOUT, **NOT UNDERNEATH.**

A FRILLED SHARK'S **BODY** IS SO **SLIM** THAT IT **RESEMBLES** A **SNAKE.**

THE **TEETH** ARE **ALIGNED** IN ABOUT **30 ROWS.** EACH **TOOTH** HAS **THREE CUSPS.** THE **TEETH** OF THE FRILLED SHARK ARE VERY **SIMILAR** TO THOSE OF **SHARKS** THAT LIVED **400 MILLION YEARS AGO.**

WHERE THEY LIVE

← SCALE →

Length: 6 feet

THERE IS ONLY **ONE DORSAL FIN**. THE DORSAL FIN IS **SMALLER** THAN THE **PELVIC** AND THE **ANAL FINS**.

THE **TAIL** HAS ONLY THE **UPPER LOBE**. THERE IS **NO LOWER LOBE**.

THE **PECTORAL FINS** ARE **SHORT** AND **ROUNDED**.

FRILLED SHARKS ARE **OVOVIVIPAROUS** AND CAN SPAWN UP TO **TEN PUPS**.

THE **FRILLED SHARK** **LIVES** AT **DEPTHS** OF **500** TO **4,000 FEET**.

THE SKIN **COLOR** IS **BROWN**.

WHAT THEY EAT

Small Bony Fish

Smaller Sharks

Cephalopods like Squid

BLUNTNOSE SIXGILL SHARK

Hexanchus griseus

Order Hexanchiformes (Sixgill and Sevengill Sharks)
Family Hexanchidae (Sixgill and Sevengill Sharks)

BLUNTNOSE SIXGILL SHARKS HAVE **18 UPPER** AND **12 BOTTOM TEETH**. EACH UPPER TOOTH IS **SERRATED** AND HAS **ONE CUSP**. THE **BOTTOM** TEETH ARE **SAW-LIKE** AND ARE SHAPED LIKE A **COMB**.

THE **EYES** ARE **BIG, GREEN,** AND **TRANSLUCENT**. THEY HAVE **ADAPTED** TO THE **DARK** AND **DEEP WATERS** WHERE THE **BLUNTNOSE SIXGILL SHARK** SPENDS THE **DAY** AND FOR **HUNTING** AT **NIGHT**.

THE **BODY** IS **STOUT**.

THE **HEAD** IS **FLAT** AND **BIG**.

BLUNTNOSE SIXGILL SHARKS HAVE **SIX GILL SLITS** ON **EACH SIDE** OF THEIR **HEADS**.

THE **MOUTH** IS POSITIONED **UNDERNEATH** THE **HEAD**.

BLUNTNOSE SIXGILL SHARKS HAVE ONLY **ONE DORSAL FIN** VERY **CLOSE** TO THE **TAIL**.

THE SKIN **COLOR** IS BROWNISH-GREY, FADING TO A **LIGHTER GREY** ON THE **BELLY**. THERE ARE **TWO LIGHT STRIPES** ON THE **SIDES**.

BLUNTNOSE SIXGILL SHARKS ARE **VERTICAL MIGRATORS.** THIS MEANS THAT, DURING THE **DAY,** THEY STAY NEAR THE **BOTTOM** OF THE **SEA,** BUT THEY **MIGRATE** TO THE **SURFACE** AT **NIGHT.**

BLUNTNOSE SIXGILL SHARKS ARE **NOCTURNAL.** THEY MIGRATE TO THE SURFACE TO **HUNT** FOR **PREY** AT NIGHT.

NOT MUCH IS KNOWN ABOUT THIS SHARK BECAUSE IT SPENDS MOST OF ITS DAY IN **VERY DEEP WATERS.** BUT IT HAS BEEN REPORTED THAT THE BLUNTNOSE SIXGILL SHARK COULD LIVE OVER **80 YEARS.**

THE **SHARKS** OF THIS **FAMILY** ARE ALSO KNOWN AS **COW SHARKS** BECAUSE OF THEIR **SIZE.**

BLUNTNOSE SIXGILL SHARKS LIVE IN **VERY DEEP** WATERS AT ABOUT **6,000 FEET.**

THE LATIN NAME **HEXANCHUS** MEANS **"SIX GILLS,"** WHILE **GRISEUS** MEANS **"GREY."** THE **ROUNDED SNOUT** INSPIRED THE COMMON NAME **BLUNTNOSE.**

BLUNTNOSE SIXGILL SHARKS ARE **OVOVIVIPAROUS** AND A **LITTER** CAN YIELD **100 PUPS,** EACH OVER **TWO FEET LONG!**

IT'S A **SLUGGISH** SHARK, BUT IT **REACTS** EXTREMELY **FAST** WHEN IT'S **HUNTING.**

←SCALE→

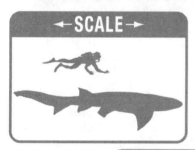

WHERE THEY LIVE

Length: 15 feet; Weight: 450 lbs. (females are bigger than males)

WHAT THEY EAT

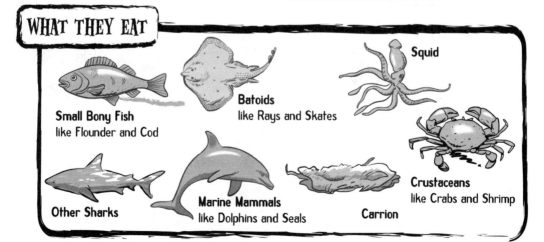

Squid

Small Bony Fish like Flounder and Cod

Batoids like Rays and Skates

Crustaceans like Crabs and Shrimp

Other Sharks

Marine Mammals like Dolphins and Seals

Carrion

BROADNOSE SEVENGILL SHARK

Notorynchus cepedianus

Order Hexanchiformes (Sixgill and Sevengill Sharks)
Family Hexanchidae (Sixgill and Sevengill Sharks)

THE BROADNOSE
SEVENGILL SHARK
HAS **SMALL EYES**
AND A **LARGE,
ROUNDED SNOUT.**

THE **UPPER TEETH**
ARE **SAW-LIKE;** THE
BOTTOM TEETH
LOOK LIKE A **COMB.**

BROADNOSE SEVENGILL
SHARKS HAVE **SEVEN GILL
SLITS** ON EACH SIDE OF
THEIR HEADS.

IT'S A **VERY RARE** AND
AGGRESSIVE SHARK.

← SCALE →

WHERE THEY LIVE

BROADNOSE SEVENGILL SHARKS SPEND MOST OF THEIR TIME AT **DEPTHS** OF **550 FEET,** SURFACING SPORADICALLY.

THE **SKIN** IS **DARK GREY,** FADING TO **LIGHTER GREY** ON THE **BELLY,** WITH **BLACK** AND **WHITE SPOTS** ON THE **BACK.**

THERE'S ONLY **ONE DORSAL FIN** LOCATED NEAR THE **TAIL.**

BROADNOSE SEVENGILL SHARKS **HUNT** IN **PACKS.** THEY CAN **HERD** A SCHOOL OF **FISH** AND THEN **DASH** INTO IT, **GRABBING** THEIR **PREY.**

THEY SPAWN **80 PUPS,** EACH **ONE** AND A **HALF FEET LONG.**

THE BROADNOSE SEVENGILL IS A **SLOW-SWIMMING SHARK,** BUT IT CAN SUDDENLY **DASH** TO **GRAB** A **PREY.**

Length: 10 feet

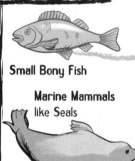

WHAT THEY EAT

Small Bony Fish

Marine Mammals
like Seals

Batoids
like Rays

Carrion

Other Sharks

SHARK BITEs!

13. WHAT DO YOU **SAY** WHEN THERE'S A BIG **STORM** OVER THE **OCEAN?**

—"IT'S RAINING **CATSHARKS** AND **DOGFISH!**"

14. WHAT DID THE **SHARK LIBRARIAN** SAY?

—"SHHH-ARK!"

QUIET!

15. WHAT KIND OF **RESTAURANT** IS **DANGEROUS** TO EAT AT?

—ONE WITH SHARK-INFESTED **WAITERS!**

The Mysterious Sharks' Tongues

In ancient times, people thought that fossilized shark teeth were tongues.

Fossils form when the bones and teeth of dead animals are replaced by minerals. Sharks' skeletons are made of cartilage, a substance that rarely becomes fossilized. But sharks' teeth are made of a stronger material. In addition, sharks shed and replace their teeth throughout their life, so fossilized sharks' teeth are easy to find. People have known about sharks' fossilized teeth since ancient times, but until recently, they had no idea what fossils really were.

There are many old theories that have tried to explain the nature of fossils and fossilized sharks' teeth. Here are some.

Aristotle (384–322 BC) was an ancient Greek philosopher and the teacher of Alexander the Great. On the subject of fossils, Aristotle theorized that there were two kinds of gasses spontaneously exhaling from the earth, smokes and vapors. When smokes solidified, they would become metals, and when vapors solidified, they would become fossils.

Pliny the Elder (23–79) was an ancient Roman Natural Philosopher. Natural philosophers were people who studied nature in ancient times. Pliny the Elder explained that fossilized sharks teeth were tongues made of stone, or, as he used to call them, "glossopetrae."

Pliny thought that glossopetrae fell from the sky during lunar eclipses and had magic powers. Pliny also claimed that glossopetrae were necessary during selenomancy, the practice of predicting the future observing the phases of the moon.

During the Middle Ages, glossopetrae were thought to be petrified snakes tongues. They were used to guard against poisons and the bite of poisonous snakes. This belief spread from a legend from the island of Malta.

The legend narrates that, on his trip to Rome, Saint Paul was shipwrecked on the island of Malta. While the few survivors were lighting a small fire to warm themselves up, a snake bit Saint Paul. In that instant, the snake tongue turned into stone, but the saint was unharmed. That's why the many fossilized sharks' teeth found on the island of Malta were thought to be petrified snakes' tongues.

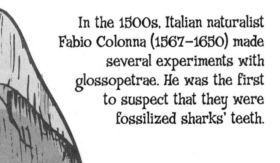

In the 1500s, Italian naturalist Fabio Colonna (1567–1650) made several experiments with glossopetrae. He was the first to suspect that they were fossilized sharks' teeth.

Fossilized tooth from a great white shark.

In 1666, a Danish anatomist called Nicolaus Steno was given an unusual present. It was the head of a huge shark just fished off the Mediterranean sea. Steno immediately noticed the similarities between the glossopetrae and the teeth of the shark. He concluded that they were the same thing, ending the centuries-long debate of what glossopetrae really were. But Steno became famous for another discovery he made while studying the shark's head, and for this he is considered the father of geology. Check it out on the next page.

A Mystery is Solved!

Niels Steensen (1638-1686) was a Danish anatomist who left Copenhagen to move to Florence, Italy. There, he changed his name to Nicolaus Steno. His mentor was Ferdinand II, the Grand Duke of Tuscany. It was Ferdinand who, upon hearing of some fishermen having captured a huge shark in the Mediterranean Sea, ordered its head to be given to Steno for research.

Steno published the results of his research in 1667. He had noticed the similarities between glossopetrae and sharks' teeth, and concluded they were the same thing. But a question remained unanswered: if sharks live in the sea, why were sharks' teeth found embedded in rocks, sometimes in caves, or up on mountains?

The shark head studied by Steno.

To answer this question, Steno came up with a brand new theory that became the basis of modern geology. He thought that the Earth must have gone through many changes. What now is above water could have been at the bottom of the ocean many centuries before. This revolutionary thought explained why sharks' teeth are found in odd places. Steno also realized that the oldest fossils are found in the lower layers of the earth. The more recent fossils are found in the upper layers. And so, thanks to a shark, Steno was able to establish the basis of modern geology.

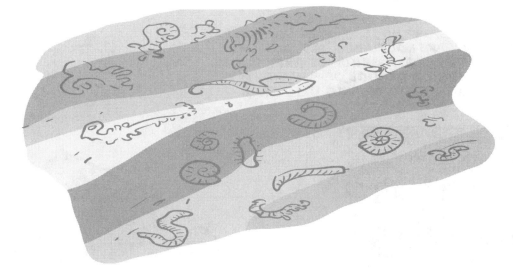

As R. Aidan Martin, director of the ReefQuest Centre for Shark Research, mentions, Steno also noted the pores on the shark's snout. He asked one of his pupils, Stefano Lorenzini, to investigate what they might be. Lorenzini described the pores and their content in detail. In fact, he even gave them his name, the ampullae of Lorenzini.

The ampullae of Lorenzini are one of the shark's senses. Every living organism emits a low electrical field and the ampullae are able to detect it. This means that if a prey is hiding under the sand, the shark is able to find it even if it can't be seen. At the time of Lorenzini there was no knowledge of electricity and the purpose of the ampullae remained a mystery.

It was only in 1967, almost 300 years later, that Sven Dijkgraaf and his pupil Adrianus Kalmijn were able to fully explain the function of the ampullae of Lorenzini.

GREY NURSE SHARK

Carcharias taurus

Order Lamniformes (Mackerel Sharks)
Family Odontaspididae (Sand Tiger Sharks)

GREY NURSE SHARKS ARE SLUGGISH ANIMALS THAT SPEND MOST OF THEIR DAY HIDING IN CAVES. THEY ARE NOCTURNAL AND, AT NIGHT, OFTEN HUNT IN PACKS. A GROUP OF GREY NURSE SHARKS CAN HERD A SCHOOL OF FISH TIGHTLY TOGETHER. THEN, THEY DIVE INTO IT TO GRAB THEIR PREY.

GREY NURSE SHARKS ARE GENERALLY NOT AGGRESSIVE AND HAVE BEEN SPEARFISHED ALMOST TO EXTINCTION IN AUSTRALIA. THEY WERE THE FIRST SHARKS TO BECOME A PROTECTED SPECIES IN 1984.

THE TWO DORSAL FINS AND THE ANAL FIN ARE SIMILAR IN SIZE.

THE SKIN COLOR IS BROWNISH-GREY, FADING TO LIGHT TAN ON THE BELLY.

← SCALE →

Length: 10 feet

WHERE THEY LIVE

GREY NURSE SHARKS ARE **OVOVIVIPAROUS**, AND THE **EGGS** HATCH INSIDE THE **FEMALE'S BODY**. IN THE FEMALE'S UTERUS, THERE'S NO **PLACENTA** TO FEED THE **EMBRYOS**. TO SURVIVE, THE EMBRYOS EAT THE **UNHATCHED EGGS**, AND THEN EACH OTHER. THE GREY NURSE SHARK FEMALE HAS **TWO UTERI**, TO PREVENT THE **LAST TWO REMAINING EMBRYOS** FROM EATING EACH OTHER. GREY NURSE SHARKS GIVE **BIRTH** TO **TWO PUPS** AFTER A **GESTATION PERIOD** OF **NINE MONTHS**. PUPS ARE OVER **THREE FEET LONG** AT BIRTH.

TO KEEP FROM **SINKING**, SHARKS NEED TO **CONSTANTLY SWIM**. BUT **GREY NURSE SHARKS** FIGURED OUT A **TRICK**. THEY COME TO THE **SURFACE** TO **SWALLOW** SOME **AIR**. THEY KEEP SOME IN THEIR **STOMACH** AND **FART** OUT THE REST. BY **CONTROLLING** THE **AMOUNT OF AIR** THEY KEEP IN THEIR STOMACH, GREY NURSE SHARKS CAN **HOVER** MOTIONLESS AT THE **DESIRED DEPTHS**.

THE **SNOUT** IS **POINTY** AND IN THE **SHAPE** OF A **CONE**.

THE **BODY** IS **STOUT**.

THE **TEETH** ARE **POINTY** AND ARE **VISIBLE** EVEN WHEN THE **MOUTH** IS **CLOSED**. THIS GIVES THE **GREY NURSE SHARK** A **FEARSOME APPEARANCE**.

GREY NURSE SHARKS LIVE NEAR THE **COASTS** AT DEPTHS OF **500 FEET**. THEY **MIGRATE** TO **COLDER WATERS** DURING THE **SUMMER**.

Shark Tales: The oil extracted from the liver of the grey nurse shark was used to light street lamps before the invention of electricity.

WHAT THEY EAT

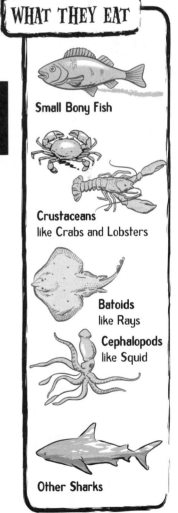

Small Bony Fish

Crustaceans
like Crabs and Lobsters

Batoids
like Rays

Cephalopods
like Squid

Other Sharks

CROCODILE SHARK

Pseudocarcharias kamoharai

Order Lamniformes (Mackerel Sharks)
Family Pseudocarchariidae (Crocodile Sharks)

THE COMMON NAME **CROCODILE** WAS INSPIRED BY THE **SHAPE** OF THIS **SHARK'S TEETH** THAT ARE SIMILAR TO THOSE OF A **CROCODILE**.

THE **EYES** ARE **BIG**.

WHEN IT'S **CAUGHT**, IT CAN **BITE VERY HARD**.

THE **GILL SLITS** ARE **LONG** AND **REACH** THE **TOP** OF THE **HEAD**.

THE **COLOR** IS **DARK GREY** WITH **WHITE SPOTS** ON TOP, FADING TO **LIGHTER GREY** ON THE **BELLY**. THE **FINS** ARE **TIPPED** WITH **WHITE**.

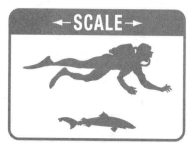
← SCALE →

Length: 3 feet
Weight: 10 lbs.

WHERE THEY LIVE

WHAT THEY EAT

Small Bony Fish

Squid

Crustaceans

CROCODILE SHARKS ARE **OVOVIVIPAROUS** AND THE **EGGS** HATCH INSIDE THE **FEMALE'S BODY. A LITTER** YIELDS **FOUR PUPS,** EACH **OVER ONE FOOT LONG.**

JUST LIKE GREY NURSE SHARKS, **CROCODILE SHARK FEMALES** HAVE **TWO UTERI** AND THE **EMBRYOS** EAT THE **UNHATCHED EGGS** AND **EACH OTHER** DURING THE GESTATION PERIOD. THE GREY NURSE SHARK'S **TWO UTERI** SUPPOSEDLY **PREVENT** THE **LAST TWO EMBRYOS** FROM **EATING EACH OTHER.** BUT STRANGELY ENOUGH, **CROCODILE SHARKS** GIVE BIRTH TO **FOUR PUPS, TWO FROM EACH UTERUS.** THIS MEANS THAT THE **REMAINING EMBRYOS** DON'T EAT EACH OTHER.

CROCODILE SHARKS ARE **VERTICAL MIGRATORS.** THEY COME TO THE **SURFACE** AT **NIGHT** TO **HUNT.** DURING THE **DAY,** THEY GO BACK TO **WATERS OVER 1,000 FEET.**

Shark Tales: In 1986, crocodile sharks repeatedly bit the fiber optic cables that AT&T had just laid in the Atlantic Ocean between the Canary Islands. This created many outages and forced AT&T to encase the cables. Why the crocodile sharks were biting the cables remains a mystery. Apparently, they were attracted by the electromagnetic field of the cables, mistaking them for prey. Deep-sea cable is generally laid on muddy ocean floors and it's quickly buried in mud. So crocodile sharks must have bitten the cables while they were being laid. But, during this process, cables don't emit any electricity because they are turned off. So the mystery remains!

GOBLIN SHARK

Mitsukurina owstoni

Order Lamniformes (Mackerel Sharks)
Family Mitsukurinidae (Goblin Sharks)

THE GOBLIN IS THE UGLIEST SHARK!

THE FINS ARE ROUNDED.

THE COLOR IS PALE PINK DUE TO A MYRIAD OF CAPILLARIES RUNNING JUST UNDER ITS SKIN. THE FINS ARE BLUE.

THE TAIL DOESN'T HAVE A LOWER LOBE.

WHAT THEY EAT

Small Bony Fish

Squid

Crustaceans

WHERE THEY LIVE

Goblin sharks have been caught in scattered spots in the Atlantic and Pacific Oceans.

Shark Tales: The first person to catch this shark was a Japanese fisherman. He immediately dubbed it "tenguzame," which means "goblin."

THE **SNOUT** IS **LONG, FLAT,** AND **POINTY.** IT MIGHT LOOK LIKE A **HORN** BUT IT'S ACTUALLY **SOFT.**

THE **AMPULLAE** OF **LORENZINI** ARE POSITIONED **UNDER** THE **SNOUT.**

THE **MOUTH** CAN **PROTRUDE** FROM **UNDER** THE **EYES** TO BEYOND THE **SNOUT.**

THE **TEETH** IN THE **FRONT** PART OF THE MOUTH ARE **LONG, THIN,** AND LOOK LIKE **FANGS.** THE **TEETH** IN THE **BACK** OF THE MOUTH ARE MUCH **SMALLER.** THEY ARE USED TO **CRUSH** THE **SHELL** OF ITS **PREY.**

THE **BODY** IS **SOFT** AND **FLABBY** LIKE MANY **DEEP-DWELLING SHARKS.**

Length: 6 feet
Weight: over 400 lbs.

GOBLIN SHARKS LIVE IN **DEEP WATERS** BETWEEN **900 AND 4,000 FEET.** NOT MUCH IS KNOWN ABOUT THIS SHARK, BUT IT IS **SUSPECTED** TO BE A **VERTICAL MIGRATOR.** DURING THE DAY GOBLIN SHARKS MOVE UP AND DOWN THE **WATER COLUMN** IN A CYCLE, FOLLOWING THE **MIGRATORY MOVEMENTS** OF THEIR **PREY.**

THE **GOBLIN SHARK** IS PROBABLY A **SLUGGISH SWIMMER,** BUT IT CAN SUDDENLY **PROJECT** ITS **MOUTH** TO CATCH **FAST-MOVING PREY.**

ALL WE KNOW ABOUT THESE SHARKS HAS BEEN DEDUCTED FROM ABOUT **FIFTY ACCIDENTAL CATCHES.** GOBLIN SHARKS HAVE NEVER BEEN **OBSERVED** IN THEIR **NATURAL ENVIRONMENT.**

← SCALE →

MEGAMOUTH SHARK

Megachasma pelagios

Order Lamniformes (Mackerel Sharks)
Family Megachasmidae (Megamouth Sharks)

THE SCIENTIFIC NAME **MEGACHASMA** MEANS **"BIG SPACE."** IT **REFERS** TO THIS SHARK'S **ENORMOUS MOUTH.** THE WORD **PELAGIOS** MEANS **"OF THE SEA."**

SCIENTISTS WERE ABLE TO **TAG** A **MEGAMOUTH SHARK.** THEY LEARNED THAT DURING THE **NIGHT,** THE MEGAMOUTH SHARK **MIGRATES** TO **50 FEET** UNDER THE SURFACE, WHILE DURING THE **DAY,** IT **DESCENDS** TO **DEPTHS** OF **500 FEET.** IN THIS **VERTICAL MIGRATION** THE MEGAMOUTH FOLLOWS ITS **PREY.**

← SCALE →

WHERE THEY LIVE

So far, fewer than 30 megamouth sharks have been seen in oceans around the world. The map indicates the locations of the few sightings.

Zooplankton

Shark Tales: The first megamouth shark was caught by accident on November 15, 1976, in Hawaii, by the US Navy. Before this date, megamouth sharks were unknown.

Length: males, 12 feet; females, 15 feet
Weight: over 1,600 lbs.

MEGAMOUTH IS A **FILTER-FEEDING** SHARK, LIKE **BASKING** AND **WHALE SHARKS.** FILTER-FEEDING MEANS THAT THE SHARK **FILTERS** WATER TO **CATCH** ITS **FOOD.** SEAWATER IS **RICH** IN **MICROORGANISMS,** LIKE **SHRIMP, JELLYFISH, LARVAE,** AND **EGGS,** TOO SMALL TO BE SEEN BY THE **NAKED EYE.** WHILE SLOWLY SWIMMING, THE MEGAMOUTH **OPENS** ITS **HUGE MOUTH** AND **FILLS** IT WITH **WATER.** THEN, IT **CLOSES** ITS MOUTH, **EXPELLING** THE **WATER** THROUGH ITS **GILL SLITS.** THE **GILL RAKERS,** ORGANS POSITIONED IN THE MEGAMOUTH'S GILLS, **FILTER** THE ESCAPING WATER, **PREVENTING** THE **ZOOPLANKTON** FROM **FLOWING AWAY.**

THE **BODY** IS **STOUT** AND THE **HEAD** IS **HUGE.**

THE **SKIN COLOR** IS **DARK GREY** ON TOP, FADING TO **LIGHT GREY** ON THE **BELLY.**

THE **MOUTH** IS **TERMINAL.** THIS MEANS THAT IT IS POSITIONED IN THE **FRONT** PART OF THE **SNOUT,** NOT UNDERNEATH.

THE **SNOUT** IS **SHORT** AND **ROUND.**

THE **TEETH** ARE **NUMEROUS, SMALL,** AND **HOOK-LIKE.** THEY ARE ORGANIZED IN **50 ROWS.**

THRESHER SHARK

Alopias vulpinus

Order Lamniformes (Mackerel Sharks)
Family Alopiidae (Thresher Sharks)

THRESHER SHARKS HUNT IN **PACKS**. THE **HUGE TAIL** IS USED TO **HERD** AND SOMETIMES TO **STUN** ITS PREY. IT HAS BEEN REPORTED THAT THRESHER SHARKS USE THEIR TAIL TO CATCH **SEABIRDS**.

THE **SKIN COLOR** IS **DARK BLUISH-GREY** ON TOP, FADING SUDDENLY TO **WHITE** ON THE BELLY. THE **UNDERSIDE** OF THE **PECTORAL FINS** IS ALSO **WHITE**.

THE **FIRST DORSAL FIN** IS MUCH BIGGER THAN THE **SECOND**.

← SCALE →

THE **PECTORAL FINS** ARE **POINTY**.

WHILE **ADULT THRESHER SHARKS** LIVE IN THE OPEN OCEAN, **JUVENILES** REMAIN **CLOSE** TO THE **SHORES.** IN THIS WAY, THEY AVOID **PREDATORS.** JUVENILES VENTURE INTO THE OPEN OCEAN ONLY WHEN THEY ARE **BIG ENOUGH** TO **DEFEND THEMSELVES.**

THRESHER SHARKS CAN **JUMP CLEAR OUT** OF THE **WATER.**

A THRESHER SHARK **PUP** IS **FIVE FEET LONG** AT BIRTH. A **LITTER** CAN YIELD UP TO **SIX PUPS.**

THRESHER SHARKS' **TAILS** ARE **EXTREMELY LONG.** THEY ACCOUNT FOR **40%** OF THE **TOTAL LENGTH** OF THE THIS SHARK!

THE **UPPER LOBE** OF THE **CAUDAL FIN** IS VERY LONG. THE **LOWER LOBE** IS MUCH SHORTER.

THRESHER SHARKS LIVE BETWEEN THE **SURFACE** AND **DEPTHS** OF **OVER 1,700 FEET.**

WHERE THEY LIVE

Length: 23 feet

WHAT THEY EAT

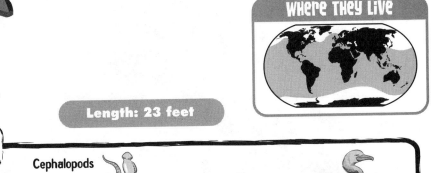

Cephalopods

Small Bony Fish

Crustaceans

Seabirds

BASKING SHARK

Cetorhinus maximus

**Order Lamniformes (Mackerel Sharks)
Family Cetorhinidae (Basking Sharks)**

THE **BASKING SHARK** IS A **FILTER-FEEDER**. IT SWIMS WITH ITS MOUTH **WIDE OPEN**, LETTING IN **SEAWATER** RICH WITH **ZOOPLANKTON**. THE WATER IS **FILTERED** BY **BRISTLE-LIKE RAKERS**, ORGANS POSITIONED IN THE BASKING SHARK'S **GILLS**. THE RAKERS **RETAIN** THE ZOOPLANKTON, WHICH IS IMMEDIATELY SWALLOWED. THE WATER IS **EXPELLED** THROUGH THE **GILLS**. A BASKING SHARK CAN FILTER **2,500 TONS** OF WATER **EVERY HOUR**.

BASKING SHARKS SWIM VERY **SLOWLY**, AT ABOUT **THREE MILES PER HOUR**. SOMETIMES THEY SWIM **BELLY UP**.

THE **GILL SLITS** ARE SO **LONG**, THEY **ENCIRCLE** THE **HEAD**.

THE BASKING SHARK'S **SKIN COLOR** IS **DARK GREY**, SLIGHTLY FADING TO A **LIGHTER GREY** ON THE BELLY.

← SCALE →

WHERE THEY LIVE

Length: 30 feet.

THE LATIN NAME **CETORHINUS MAXIMUS** MEANS "BIG WHALE-NOSED."

IT'S THE **SECOND BIGGEST SHARK** AND CAN WEIGH **FOUR** AND A **HALF TONS!** DESPITE ITS HUGE SIZE, THE BASKING SHARK FEEDS ON ONE OF THE SMALLEST FOOD, **ZOOPLANKTON!**

THE **SNOUT** IS **POINTY.**

BASKING SHARKS SWIM IN **GROUPS** OF **TWO** OR **THREE,** CLOSE TO THE **SURFACE,** GENERALLY WITH THEIR **MOUTHS OPEN.** SOMETIMES THEY FORM **GROUPS** OF 100 INDIVIDUALS.

A **PUP** IS **SIX FEET LONG** AT BIRTH. THE **GESTATION PERIOD** IS SUSPECTED TO BE **THREE** AND A **HALF YEARS LONG!** THAT'S LONGER THAN **ELEPHANTS.**

DESPITE THE **HUGE SIZE,** BASKING SHARKS ARE NOT **AGGRESSIVE.**

IT HAS BEEN REPORTED THAT BASKING SHARKS FEED ON ZOOPLANKTON ONLY DURING THE **SPRING** AND **SUMMER.** DURING THE **FALL** AND **WINTER,** BASKING SHARKS **SHED** THEIR **GILL RAKERS** AND **HIBERNATE** AT THE **BOTTOM** OF THE **OCEAN.**

ANOTHER THEORY IS THAT BASKING SHARKS **MIGRATE** TO **WARMER WATERS** DURING THE **WINTER.** BUT NOT MUCH IS KNOWN ABOUT THEIR **MIGRATIONS.**

BASKING SHARKS HAVE **NUMEROUS,** AND **USELESS, HOOK-LIKE TEETH.** THESE SHARKS DON'T USE THEIR TEETH TO CATCH **ZOOPLANKTON.**

WHAT THEY EAT

Small Bony Fish

Zooplankton

Zooplankton is the collective name of many diverse animals that live in the water. They are too small to be seen by the naked eye.

Zooplankton can contain small crustaceans, jellyfish, invertebrates, worms, fish eggs, and larvae.

GREAT WHITE SHARK

Carcharodon carcharias

Order Lamniformes (Mackerel Sharks)
Family Lamnidae (Mackerel Sharks)

THE **GREAT WHITE SHARK** IS KNOWN BY MANY **AWE-INSPIRING NAMES** SUCH AS **WHITE POINTER, WHITE-DEATH,** AND **MAN-EATER.** THE LATIN NAME COMES FROM GREEK WORDS AND MEANS **"SHARP-TOOTHED POINTER."** GREAT WHITES ARE THE **BIGGEST PREDATORY FISH.**

THE **SKIN COLOR** IS **GREY,** FADING TO **WHITE.** THE **PECTORAL FINS** MAY BE **BLACK-TIPPED.**

← SCALE →

ONE THEORY SUGGESTS THAT GREAT WHITES DESCEND FROM **MEGALODON,** A **HUGE PREDATOR** NOW EXTINCT. BUT RECENTLY, A **NEW THEORY** CLAIMS THAT THE GREAT WHITE HAS **EVOLVED** FROM THE SAME **ANCESTOR** THAT SPAWNED **MAKO SHARKS.** BOTH THEORIES SEEM TO AGREE THAT THE **FIRST GREAT WHITE SHARKS** APPEARED IN THE **MIOCENE EPOCH, 20 MILLION YEARS AGO.**

DESPITE ITS **HUGE BODY,** A GREAT WHITE CAN **JUMP** CLEAR OUT OF THE **WATER.** IT HAS BEEN KNOWN TO **SUMMERSAULT** AND TO **JUMP** FROM THE WATER INTO A **BOAT.**

Length: **14 feet**
Life span: **15 years**

THE **SNOUT** IS **SHORT** AND **POINTY.**

GREAT WHITES' **UPPER TEETH** ARE **BIG, TRIANGULAR,** AND **SERRATED.** THEY ARE USED TO **BITE** AND **CRUSH** THE **PREY.** THE **BOTTOM TEETH** HAVE THE SAME **CHARACTERISTICS,** BUT ARE **THINNER** THAN THE UPPER TEETH. THEY ARE USED TO **HOLD** THE **PREY STILL.** THE **GREAT WHITES' BITE** AND **TEETH** ARE SO **POWERFUL,** THEY CAN **CUT** THROUGH A **SEAL** AND **CRUSH** THE **SHELL** OF A **TURTLE!**

WHERE THEY LIVE

GREAT WHITE SHARK

GREAT WHITES GIVE BIRTH **EVERY OTHER YEAR,** AFTER A **GESTATION PERIOD** OF **ONE YEAR.** WHILE STILL IN THEIR MOTHER'S WOMB, THE **EMBRYOS** ARE KNOWN TO **SWALLOW** AND **DIGEST** THE **TEETH** THAT THEY **SHED.** THEY **RECYCLE** THE **CALCIUM** AND **OTHER MINERALS** TO **BUILD** UP **NEW TEETH.**

A **LITTER** CAN YIELD **TEN PUPS.** A PUP IS **FOUR** AND A **HALF FEET LONG** AT BIRTH. PUPS ARE BORN BETWEEN **SPRING** AND **SUMMER.**

THE **SECOND DORSAL FIN** IS **PUNY.**

GREAT WHITE **JUVENILES** FEED MOSTLY ON **BONY FISH.** ONCE THEY BECOME **ADULTS** THEY INCLUDE **MARINE MAMMALS** IN THEIR **DIET.**

GREAT WHITES LIVE **CLOSE** TO THE **SHORELINE,** BETWEEN THE **SURFACE** AND **DEPTHS** OF **800 FEET.**

GREAT WHITES ARE ABLE TO MAKE **TRANS-OCEANIC JOURNEYS,** SWIMMING **20 MILES A DAY.**

GREAT WHITES ARE **SOLITARY ANIMALS** THAT GENERALLY DON'T **INTERACT** WITH EACH OTHER. IF TWO GREAT WHITE SHARKS **MEET,** THEY **TURN AWAY,** SWIMMING IN **OPPOSITE DIRECTIONS.** OTHER TIMES, THEY SWIM **PARALLEL** TO **EACH OTHER** FOR A WHILE, BEFORE **TURNING AWAY.** THEY SEEM TO BE **GUARDING** THEIR **PERSONAL SPACE** FROM OTHER GREAT WHITE SHARKS.

THE GREAT WHITE SHARK IS AN **ENDANGERED SPECIES** AND IT'S **PROTECTED** IN SEVERAL PLACES LIKE **SOUTH AFRICA, FLORIDA, CALIFORNIA, NAMIBIA, THE MALDIVES,** AND **AUSTRALIA.**

FISH, AMPHIBIANS, AND REPTILES ARE COLD-BLOODED ANIMALS. THEY RELY ON AN OUTSIDE HEAT SOURCE TO MAINTAIN THEIR BODY TEMPERATURE. IF THE OUTSIDE TEMPERATURE DROPS TOO LOW, THESE ANIMALS BECOME SLUGGISH AND AREN'T ABLE TO FULLY FUNCTION.

MAMMALS CAN MAINTAIN A CONSTANT BODY TEMPERATURE BECAUSE THEY CAN GENERATE THEIR OWN HEAT. WITHIN CERTAIN BOUNDARIES, MAMMALS ARE ABLE TO FUNCTION INDEPENDENTLY FROM THE OUTSIDE TEMPERATURE.

ALTHOUGH COLD-BLOODED, SOME SHARKS, LIKE GREAT WHITES AND MAKOS, ARE ABLE TO MODIFY THEIR BODY TEMPERATURE. THIS ABILITY ALLOWS THEM TO SWIM EXTREMELY QUICKLY IN SHORT BURSTS.

THE GREAT WHITE IS CONSIDERED EXTREMELY DANGEROUS. IT HAS BEEN RESPONSIBLE FOR MANY ATTACKS ON PEOPLE, SEVERAL OF WHICH WERE FATAL.

ONE THEORY SUGGESTS THAT MANY OF THE GREAT WHITES NON-FATAL ATTACKS ON PEOPLE WERE A CASE OF MISTAKEN IDENTITY. THIS MEANS THAT THE SHARK INITIALLY MISTOOK THE VICTIM FOR A PREY, BUT, AFTER THE FIRST EXPLORATORY BITE, KNEW IT WASN'T AND LET IT GO.

ANOTHER THEORY SUGGESTS THAT GREAT WHITES DON'T NEED TO BITE TO RECOGNIZE PREY, BECAUSE THEY CAN VISUALLY DISTINGUISH PREY FROM A PERSON. THE BITING COULD BE A WARNING THAT THE SHARK'S PERSONAL SPACE WAS INVADED.

WHEN A GREAT WHITE IS READY TO ATTACK, IT SHOWS ITS TEETH, LIKE A DOG, ARCHES ITS BACK, AND KEEPS ITS PECTORAL FINS POINTING DOWN.

GREAT WHITE SHARK

THE GREAT WHITE IS AN **APEX PREDATOR.**
THIS MEANS THAT THERE'S **NO ANIMAL** THAT
HUNTS AND **EATS** GREAT WHITES.

THE GREAT WHITE IS A **SKILLED HUNTER.** IT **LURKS** IN DEEP WATERS, WAITING FOR A **VICTIM** TO SWIM BY ON THE **SURFACE.** WHEN ONE PASSES BY, THE GREAT WHITE QUICKLY SWIMS **VERTICALLY UP** AND **BITES** THE **UNSUSPECTING PREY.** THEN, THE SHARK SWIMS AWAY, WHILE ITS VICTIM **WEAKENS** OR **DIES** FROM THE **SHOCK** AND **LOSS** OF **BLOOD.** FINALLY, THE GREAT WHITE **COMES BACK TO FEAST** ON THE **CARCASS.** THE GREAT WHITE WINS ITS **MEAL** WITH **LITTLE EFFORT** AND **NO STRUGGLE.**

OTHER TIMES, THE GREAT WHITE SWIMS ALONG **DIRECTLY BENEATH** ITS PREY. SUDDENLY, IT **HEADS UPWARDS** AND, ON REACHING ITS TARGET, **WHIPS** ITS **HEAD UP** AND **SNAPS** AT ITS PREY.

THE **BIGGEST GREAT WHITE** WARNS THE OTHER GREAT WHITES TO **STAY AWAY** FROM ITS **FOOD.** IT ACCOMPLISHES THIS BY **SPLASHING** AND **HITTING** THEM WITH ITS **TAIL.**

GREAT WHITE SHARKS OFTEN THRASH **FISHERMEN NETS** TO STEAL THE **FISH.** BUT SOMETIMES THEY GET **CAUGHT** IN THEM.

THIS SHARK DOESN'T LIKE **SEA OTTERS** AND **SEABIRDS** AS MUCH. WHEN IT CATCHES THEM, THE GREAT WHITE **RELEASES** THEM, OFTEN WITH ONLY **MINOR BRUISES.**

GREAT WHITES HAVE BEEN OBSERVED "**BOUNCING SEABIRDS.**" WHEN A SEABIRD SITS ON THE **SURFACE,** THE SHARK **SWIMS** FROM **UNDERNEATH.** THEN, IT **HITS** THE **UNSUSPECTING SEABIRD** WITH ITS **SNOUT.** THE MEANING OF THIS BEHAVIOR IS **UNKNOWN.** MAYBE THE GREAT WHITES ARE JUST **PLAYING AROUND.**

WHAT THEY EAT

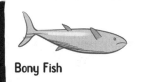

Bony Fish

Sea Turtles

Crustaceans
like Crabs

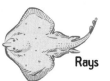

Rays

Marine Mammals
like Dolphins, Seals,
and Sea Lions

Cephalopods
like Octopi

Other Sharks

Carcasses of Marine Mammals.
Great whites are particularly fond
of whales' fat-rich blubber. Blubber
is a thick layer of fat that insulates
marine mammals.

SHORTFIN MAKO

Isurus oxyrinchus

Order Lamniformes (Mackerel Sharks)
Family Lamnidae (Mackerel Sharks)

SHORTFIN MAKOS ARE **KNOWN**, AND **FEARED**, IN **NEW ZEALAND**. IN FACT, THE WORD **MAKO** IS A **MAORI** WORD. THE **MAORIS** ARE THE **NATIVE PEOPLE** OF **NEW ZEALAND**. FOR THE MAORIS, **MAKO** MEANS "MAN-EATER."

DESPITE THE **BAD REPUTATION** WITH THE MAORIS, SHORTFIN MAKOS ARE NOT **DANGEROUS** UNLESS **PROVOKED**.

THE SHORTFIN MAKO IS **SHAPED** LIKE A **SPINDLE**. THIS **CHARACTERISTIC** MAKES THE MAKO **HYDRODYNAMIC** AND **FAST**.

SHORTFIN MAKOS ARE **SOLITARY SHARKS**.

MAKOS CAN **SKILLFULLY JUMP** OUT OF THE **WATER**.

THE **SKIN COLOR** IS **DARK BLUE** ON TOP, FADING ABRUPTLY TO **WHITE** ON THE **BELLY**.

THE **SECOND DORSAL** AND THE **ANAL FINS** ARE **PUNY**.

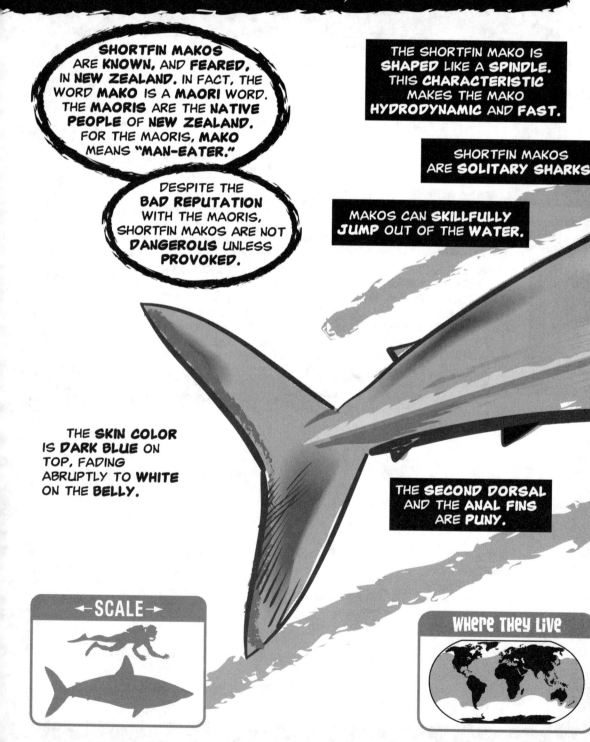

← SCALE →

WHERE THEY LIVE

ALTHOUGH **COLD-BLOODED**, THE SHORTFIN MAKO IS ABLE TO **RAISE** ITS BODY **TEMPERATURE**. IN THIS WAY, MAKOS CAN SWIM **EXTREMELY FAST** IN **FRIGID WATERS**.

THE SHORTFIN MAKO IS THE **FASTEST** OF ALL SHARKS. IT CAN REACH A **SPEED** OF **20 MILES** PER **HOUR**. THIS MIGHT NOT SEEM MUCH, BUT THE **AVERAGE OLYMPIC ATHLETE** SWIMS AT A SPEED OF ONLY **4 MILES** PER **HOUR!**

THIS SHARK CAN MAKE **TRANS-OCEANIC JOURNEYS** AND TRAVEL AT AN AVERAGE OF **35 MILES PER DAY**.

THE **EYES** ARE **VERY BIG**.

THE **SNOUT** IS **VERY POINTY**.

THE **TEETH** ARE **HOOK-LIKE** AND **SMOOTH,** NOT SERRATED.

THE **SHORTFIN** AND THE **LONGFIN MAKOS** (ISURUS PAUCUS) ARE VERY **SIMILAR**. THE **LONGFIN MAKO** HAS **LARGER EYES** AND, AS THE **COMMON NAME** IMPLIES, **LONGER PECTORAL FINS**.

A **LITTER** CAN SPAWN UP TO **20 PUPS**.

Length: 8 feet
Weight: 250 lbs.

WHAT THEY EAT

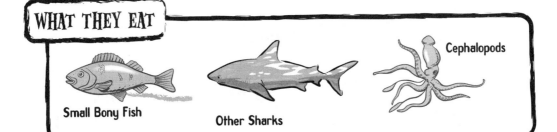

Small Bony Fish

Other Sharks

Cephalopods

PORBEAGLE SHARK

Lamna nasus

Order Lamniformes (Mackerel Sharks)
Family Lamnidae (Mackerel Sharks)

THE **FIRST DORSAL FIN** HAS A **WHITE FREE REAR TIP.**

THE **EYES** ARE **VERY BIG** AND **BLACK.**

THE **SNOUT** IS **VERY POINTY.**

THE **BODY** IS **STOUT** AND **TORPEDO-SHAPED.**

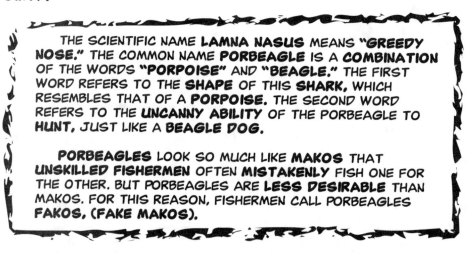

THE SCIENTIFIC NAME **LAMNA NASUS** MEANS **"GREEDY NOSE."** THE COMMON NAME **PORBEAGLE** IS A **COMBINATION** OF THE WORDS **"PORPOISE"** AND **"BEAGLE."** THE FIRST WORD REFERS TO THE **SHAPE** OF THIS **SHARK,** WHICH RESEMBLES THAT OF A **PORPOISE.** THE SECOND WORD REFERS TO THE **UNCANNY ABILITY** OF THE PORBEAGLE TO **HUNT,** JUST LIKE A **BEAGLE DOG.**

PORBEAGLES LOOK SO MUCH LIKE **MAKOS** THAT **UNSKILLED FISHERMEN** OFTEN **MISTAKENLY** FISH ONE FOR THE OTHER. BUT PORBEAGLES ARE **LESS DESIRABLE** THAN MAKOS. FOR THIS REASON, FISHERMEN CALL PORBEAGLES **FAKOS,** (FAKE MAKOS).

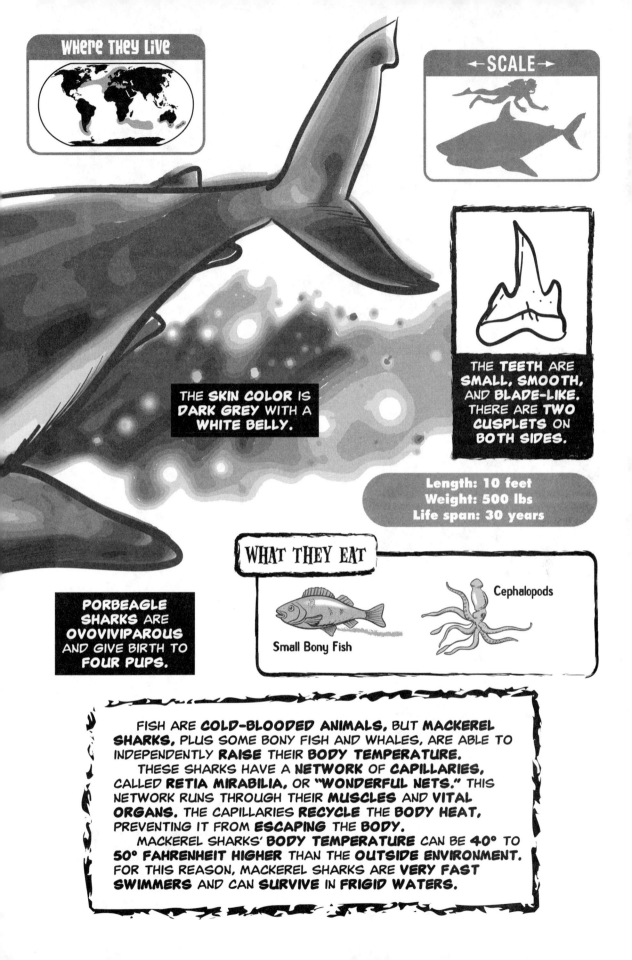

SCALE

THE **TEETH** ARE **SMALL, SMOOTH,** AND **BLADE-LIKE.** THERE ARE **TWO CUSPLETS** ON **BOTH SIDES.**

THE **SKIN COLOR** IS **DARK GREY** WITH A **WHITE BELLY.**

Length: 10 feet
Weight: 500 lbs
Life span: 30 years

WHAT THEY EAT

Cephalopods

Small Bony Fish

PORBEAGLE SHARKS ARE **OVOVIVIPAROUS** AND GIVE BIRTH TO **FOUR PUPS.**

FISH ARE **COLD-BLOODED ANIMALS,** BUT **MACKEREL SHARKS,** PLUS SOME BONY FISH AND WHALES, ARE ABLE TO INDEPENDENTLY **RAISE** THEIR **BODY TEMPERATURE.**

THESE SHARKS HAVE A **NETWORK** OF **CAPILLARIES,** CALLED **RETIA MIRABILIA,** OR **"WONDERFUL NETS."** THIS NETWORK RUNS THROUGH THEIR **MUSCLES** AND **VITAL ORGANS.** THE CAPILLARIES **RECYCLE** THE **BODY HEAT,** PREVENTING IT FROM **ESCAPING** THE **BODY.**

MACKEREL SHARKS' **BODY TEMPERATURE** CAN BE **40°** TO **50° FAHRENHEIT HIGHER** THAN THE **OUTSIDE ENVIRONMENT.** FOR THIS REASON, MACKEREL SHARKS ARE **VERY FAST SWIMMERS** AND CAN **SURVIVE** IN **FRIGID WATERS.**

NECKLACE CARPETSHARK

Parascyllium variolatum

Order Orectolobiformes (Carpetsharks)
Family Parascylliidae (Collared Carpetsharks)

THE **SKIN COLOR** IS **DARK BROWN** WITH **WHITE SPOTS**. THERE'S A **BLACK RING** WITH **SMALLER WHITE SPOTS** AROUND THE **GILL AREA**. AS THE COMMON NAME SUGGESTS, THIS **RING** RESEMBLES A **NECKLACE**.

THE **POINTY BARBELS** ON THE **SNOUT** ARE SENSORY **ORGANS**. THEY **AID** THE NECKLACE CARPETSHARK TO **FIND** ITS **PREY**.

← SCALE →

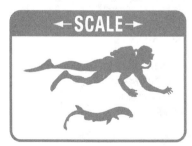

WHERE THEY LIVE

WHAT THEY EAT

Small Bony Fish

Crustaceans
like Crabs and Shrimp

Squid

THE **SKIN COLOR** HELPS THE NECKLACE CARPETSHARK TO **CAMOUFLAGE** IN ITS **ENVIRONMENT**. NECKLACE CARPETSHARKS ARE **BOTTOM-DWELLERS** AND ARE FOUND ON **ROCKY REEFS, SANDY BOTTOMS,** AND **SEAGRASS BEDS.**

Length: 3 feet

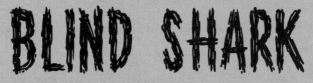

BLIND SHARK

Brachaelurus waddi

Order Orectolobiformes (Carpetsharks)
Family Brachaeluridae (Blind sharks)

BLIND SHARKS ARE NOT REALLY **BLIND**. THE COMMON NAME WAS INSPIRED BY THEIR **HABIT** OF **CLOSING** THEIR **EYES** WHEN CAUGHT.

BLIND SHARKS LIVE NEAR THE **COASTS**, AT A **DEPTH** OF **500 FEET**. THEY ARE **BOTTOM-DWELLERS**.

DURING THE **DAY**, BLIND SHARKS HIDE IN THE **CAVES** OF **ROCKY BOTTOMS** AND **CORAL REEFS**.

THE **PATTERN** ON THEIR **BACKS** AND THE **COLORS** OF THE **ENVIRONMENT** ARE **SIMILAR**, MAKING IT **HARD** FOR THEIR **PREDATORS** TO **FIND** THEM.

DURING THE **NIGHT**, BLIND SHARKS COME OUT FROM THEIR **HIDING PLACES** TO **HUNT**.

THE **TWO DORSAL FINS** ARE **SIMILAR** IN **SIZE** AND **CLOSE** TO THE **TAIL**. THEY **BOTH** HAVE A **FREE REAR TIP**.

THE **TAIL FIN** IS **SHORT** AND THE **LOWER LOBE** IS **ABSENT**.

Length: 4 feet

WHERE THEY LIVE

← SCALE →

Small Bony Fish

Crustaceans
like Crabs and Shrimp

Cephalopods
like Squid

Sea Anemones

THE **SKIN COLOR** IS **DARK BROWNISH-GREY** ON TOP, FADING TO **TAN** ON THE **BELLY**. ON THE **BACK** THERE ARE **SADDLE-SHAPED BLOTCHES** AND **LIGHT SPOTS**. THE BLOTCHES ARE **DARKER** IN **PUPS** AND **JUVENILES**, BUT TEND TO **FADE** IN **ADULTS**. THE OVERALL **PATTERN** IS NOT AS **INTRICATE** AS THAT OF THE **NECKLACE CARPETSHARK**.

THERE ARE **TWO SPIRACLES** BEHIND THE **EYES**.

THE **EYES** ARE **OVAL** AND **SMALL**. THEY **PROTRUDE** FROM THE **HEAD**.

BLIND SHARKS HAVE **TWO BARBELS** ON THEIR **SNOUT**.

ORNATE WOBBEGONG

Orectolobus ornatus

Order Orectolobiformes (Carpetsharks)
Family Orectolobidae (Wobbegongs)

THE **ORNATE WOBBEGONG'S** COMMON NAME REFERS TO THE **INTRICATE PATTERN** OF **BROWN** AND **GOLDEN BLOTCHES** AND **BLUE SPOTS** ON THE **BACK** OF THIS **SHARK.**

THIS SHARK LIVES ON **ROCKY SEAFLOORS** AND **CORAL REEFS.** THE **DORSAL PATTERN** MAKES THEM **BLEND** WITH THEIR **ENVIRONMENT,** WHICH BOTH PROTECTS THEM FROM **PREDATORS,** AND MAKES THEM **INVISIBLE** TO THEIR **PREY.**

WHERE THEY LIVE

THE **BODY** IS **BROAD** AND **FLAT.**

ORNATE WOBBEGONGS LIVE NEAR THE **SURFACE** TO **DEPTHS** OF **50 FEET.**

Shark Tales: The pattern is so attractive and the skin so tough that ornate wobbegongs are often used in the leather goods industry.

Length: 10 feet

WHAT THEY EAT

Small Bony Fish

Crustaceans like Lobsters

Cephalopods like Octopi

Cuttlefish

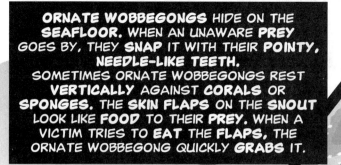

ORNATE WOBBEGONGS HIDE ON THE SEAFLOOR. WHEN AN UNAWARE PREY GOES BY, THEY SNAP IT WITH THEIR POINTY, NEEDLE-LIKE TEETH.
SOMETIMES ORNATE WOBBEGONGS REST VERTICALLY AGAINST CORALS OR SPONGES. THE SKIN FLAPS ON THE SNOUT LOOK LIKE FOOD TO THEIR PREY. WHEN A VICTIM TRIES TO EAT THE FLAPS, THE ORNATE WOBBEGONG QUICKLY GRABS IT.

← SCALE →

EPAULETTE SHARK

Hemiscyllium ocellatum

Order Orectolobiformes (Carpetsharks)
Family Hemiscylliidae (Longtailed Carpetsharks)

EPAULETTE SHARKS LIVE IN **CORAL REEFS**, WHERE THE **WATER** IS **SHALLOW**, AND IN **NATURAL WATER POOLS**.

THEY USE THEIR **PECTORAL FINS** TO **PROP** THEMSELVES **UP** AND **CLIMB** THE CORAL REEF. THESE SHARKS HAVE BEEN SEEN **CRAWLING OUT** OF THE **WATER** FROM ONE **POOL** TO **ANOTHER**.

IN **SHALLOW PONDS,** THE AMOUNT OF **OXYGEN** IN THE **WATER** IS **LOW.** TO SURVIVE, THE EPAULETTE SHARK IS ABLE TO **TURN OFF** THE **PARTS** OF ITS **BRAIN** THAT ARE NOT **NEEDED.** IN THIS WAY, IT CAN DEVOTE THE **AVAILABLE OXYGEN** TO THE **TASKS** AT **HAND.**

WHERE THEY LIVE

THE **TWO DORSAL FINS** ARE **SIMILAR** IN **SIZE** AND BOTH HAVE **FREE REAR TIPS.** THEY ARE POSITIONED **CLOSE** TO THE **TAIL.**

EPAULETTE SHARKS LAY **EGGS.** THE EGGS ARE **OVAL,** ABOUT **FOUR INCHES** BY **ONE** AND A **HALF.** A **PUP** IS **SIX INCHES LONG** AT BIRTH.

THE LATIN NAME **OCELLATUM** MEANS **"WITH EYES."** IT REFERS TO THE **TWO SPOTS**, WHICH LOOK LIKE **EYES**, POSITIONED ABOVE THE **PECTORAL FINS**. THE SPOTS ARE **STRIKINGLY BIG** AND **BLACK** WITH A **WHITE OUTLINE.**

THE **SKIN COLOR** IS **BROWN** AND **YELLOW**, WITH **SADDLE-LIKE BLOTCHES** AND **DARK SPOTS.**

WHAT THEY EAT

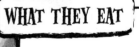

Worms

Crustaceans
like Crabs and Shrimp

← SCALE →

GREY BAMBOOSHARK

Chiloscyllium griseum

Order Orectolobiformes (Carpetsharks)
Family Hemiscylliidae (Longtailed Carpetsharks)

THE NAME **CHILOSCYLLIUM** IS COMPOSED OF TWO WORDS. **CHILO** MEANS **"LIPS"**, AND **SCYLLIUM** MEANS **"SHARK."** THE **GREY BAMBOOSHARKS** HAVE **FLESHY LIPS.**

THE WORD **GRISEUM** MEANS **"GREY."** THE **SKIN COLOR** OF THIS SHARK IS **BROWNISH-GREY** ABOVE, FADING TO **LIGHT TAN** ON THE **BELLY.**

WHAT THEY EAT

Very little is known about the grey bamboosharks' diet. It's suspected to be very similar to that of the epaulette shark.

Worms

Crustaceans
like Crabs and Shrimp

← SCALE →

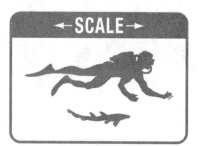

PUPS OF THIS SPECIES HAVE **BIG, BLACK** AND **WHITE BLOTCHES.** THEY **FADE** AND EVENTUALLY **DISAPPEAR** WHEN THE PUP BECOMES AN **ADULT.**

GREY BAMBOOSHARKS ARE **NOT AFRAID** OF **DIVERS** AND CAN ACTUALLY BE **CAUGHT** BY **HAND.**
LIKE THE OTHER SHARKS OF THIS FAMILY, GREY BAMBOOSHARKS CAN **SURVIVE** FOR **SEVERAL HOURS** AFTER BEING TAKEN OUT OF THE **WATER.**

THE **TWO DORSAL FINS** ARE APPROXIMATELY THE **SAME SIZE.** THEY ARE POSITIONED **CLOSE** TO THE **TAIL.**

THE **TAIL** IS **LONG** AND IS MISSING THE **LOWER LOBE.**

WHERE THEY LIVE

NURSE SHARK

Ginglymostoma cirratum

Order Orectolobiformes (Carpetsharks)
Family Ginglymostomatidae (Nurse Sharks)

THE NAME **NURSE SHARK** IS PROBABLY A VARIATION OF AN **OLD ENGLISH WORD** FOR CATSHARK, **"NUSSE."**

ANOTHER THEORY SUGGESTS THAT THE NAME **NURSE** WAS INSPIRED BY THE **NOISE** THESE SHARKS MAKE WHEN THEY ARE **CAUGHT.** SOME PEOPLE THINK THAT THEY SOUND LIKE A **BABY** BEING **NURSED.**

GINGLYMOSTOMA MEANS **"HINGED MOUTH."** IT MIGHT REFER TO THE **FLESHY SIDES** OF THIS SHARK'S **LIPS.** BUT IT COULD ALSO REFER TO THE NURSE SHARK'S **ABILITY** TO SUCK **MOLLUSKS** OUT OF THEIR **SHELLS.**

THE **TAIL** IS MISSING THE **LOWER LOBE** AND IT'S **ONE QUARTER** OF THE **TOTAL LENGTH.**

AN **ADULT** NURSE SHARK'S **SKIN COLOR** IS **BROWN.** SOMETIMES THE **TAIL** IS **WHITE** OR **BRIGHT YELLOW.** A **JUVENILE** NURSE SHARK HAS **SPOTS** ON ITS BODY, AND CAN **SLIGHTLY CHANGE** THE **COLOR** OF ITS **SKIN** TO BLEND WITH THE **ENVIRONMENT.**

Length: 8 feet
Weight: 250 lbs.

WHERE THEY LIVE

←SCALE→

DURING THE **DAY**, NURSE SHARKS CONGREGATE IN **SCHOOLS** OF **50 INDIVIDUALS** IN **SHALLOW WATERS.** THEY LAY **MOTIONLESS** ON THE **SEAFLOOR,** OR HIDE IN **CAVES,** OFTEN **PILING UP** ON **EACH OTHER.** DURING THE **NIGHT,** THE NURSE SHARK **DESCENDS** TO DEPTHS OF **300 FEET** TO **HUNT.**

LIKE MANY OF THE SHARKS IN THIS ORDER, **NURSE SHARKS** CAN **USE** THEIR **PECTORAL FINS,** ALMOST LIKE LEGS, TO CLIMB **ROCKY BOTTOMS.** THEY COME OUT OF THE WATER, **MOVING** FROM **ONE WATER POOL** TO **ANOTHER,** SEARCHING FOR **FOOD.**

THESE ARE **SLOW-MOVING SHARKS,** BUT THEY ARE STILL ABLE TO CATCH **FAST-MOVING PREY,** LIKE SMALL BONY FISH. TO ACCOMPLISH THIS, THE NURSE SHARKS QUICKLY **SUCKS IN** PREY WITH ITS **MOUTH.** NURSE SHARKS ARE ALSO ABLE TO **FLIP** SHELLS **OVER** AND **SUCK** THE ANIMAL **OUT** OF IT.

NURSE SHARKS DO NOT ATTACK PEOPLE. BUT, IF THEY FEEL **THREATENED,** THEY **BITE** SO **HARD** THAT THEIR **MOUTH** HAS TO BE **SURGICALLY FORCED OPEN!**

THE **GESTATION PERIOD** LASTS FOR **SIX MONTHS.** A **LITTER** CAN SPAWN **40 PUPS,** EACH ABOUT **ONE FOOT LONG.**

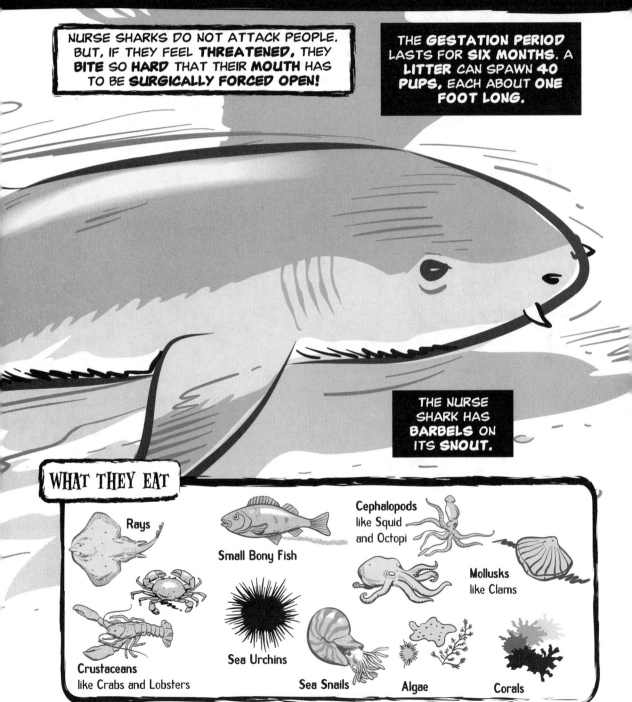

THE NURSE SHARK HAS **BARBELS** ON ITS **SNOUT.**

WHAT THEY EAT

Rays

Small Bony Fish

Cephalopods
like Squid
and Octopi

Mollusks
like Clams

Crustaceans
like Crabs and Lobsters

Sea Urchins

Sea Snails

Algae

Corals

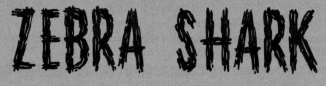

ZEBRA SHARK

Stegostoma fasciatum

Order Orectolobiformes (Carpetsharks)
Family Stegostomatidae (Zebra Sharks)

THE COMMON NAME **ZEBRA** WAS INSPIRED BY THE **STRIPED PATTERN** OF THE **JUVENILE ZEBRA SHARK'S SKIN.** UNLIKE ZEBRAS, THE YOUNG OF THIS SPECIES ARE **DARK BROWN** WITH **YELLOW STRIPES** AND **SPOTS.**

THE **AUSTRALIAN** COMMON NAME FOR THIS FISH IS **LEOPARD SHARK.** THE **PATTERN** ON THE **ADULT** ZEBRA SHARK IS **YELLOWISH-BROWN** WITH **BLACK SPOTS,** SIMILAR TO THAT OF A **LEOPARD.**

THE **TWO DORSAL FINS** ARE **CLOSE** TO EACH OTHER.

THE **CAUDAL FIN** DOESN'T HAVE THE **LOWER LOBE.** IT'S VERY LONG, **HALF** THE **TOTAL LENGTH** OF THE **SHARK.**

A zebra shark pup with the characteristic zebra-like stripes.

← SCALE →

WHERE THEY LIVE

Length: 10 feet
Life span: 10 years

ZEBRA SHARKS ARE **OVIPAROUS** AND LAY **EGGS**. THE EGGS ARE ABOUT **SEVEN INCHES LONG** AND **TWO INCHES WIDE**.

THE EGGS ARE **BROWN** AND **PURPLE**, WITH **YELLOW FRINGES**. ZEBRA SHARKS **HOOK** THEM TO **CORALS** AND **ALGAE**, WHERE IT'S **HARD** FOR **PREDATORS** TO **FIND** THEM.

A **PUP** IS **EIGHT INCHES** LONG.

ZEBRA SHARKS **LIVE** FOR ABOUT **10 YEARS** IN THE **WILD**, AND OVER **25** IN **CAPTIVITY**.

THESE SHARKS LIVE IN **CORAL REEFS** BETWEEN **SHALLOW WATERS** AND **DEPTHS** OF **200 FEET**.

THERE ARE **RIDGES** ALONG THE **ZEBRA SHARK'S BODY**.

THE **SPIRACLES** ARE AS **BIG** AS THE **EYES**.

THERE ARE **BARBELS** ON THE **SNOUT**.

ZEBRA SHARKS HAVE **FIVE GILLS** AND **FOUR GILL SLITS**. THE **FOURTH** AND **FIFTH GILL** SHARE ONE **OPENING**.

WHAT THEY EAT

Sea Snails

Crustaceans like Crabs and Shrimp

Shellfish

Small Bony Fish

WHALE SHARK

Rhincodon typus

Order Orectolobiformes (Carpetsharks)
Family Rhincodontidae (Whale Sharks)

THE LATIN NAME **RHINCODON** COMES FROM THE GREEK AND MEANS **"FILING TOOTH."** IT REFERS TO THE **TINY, HOOK-LIKE TEETH** OF THE WHALE SHARK.

THE COMMON NAME **WHALE SHARK** WAS GIVEN TO THIS **ENORMOUS FISH** BECAUSE OF ITS **SIZE.** WHALE SHARKS ARE OVER **65 FEET LONG!** THEY ARE THE **BIGGEST FISH** AND THE **BIGGEST SHARKS,** BUT THEY ARE **NOT WHALES.** THE **BLUE WHALE,** WHICH IS A **MARINE MAMMAL,** IS **BIGGER** THAN THE **WHALE SHARK.**

THE **TEETH** ARE **VERY SMALL.** THERE ARE **OVER 3,000 TEETH** INSIDE A WHALE SHARK'S **MOUTH.**

THE **MOUTH** IS **VERY LARGE** AND IN **FRONT** OF THE **SNOUT.** THE **MOUTH** IS **FOUR FEET LONG!**

THE **EYES** ARE **PUNY.**

THE **HEAD** IS **FLAT.**

THE **GILL SLITS** ARE **VERY LONG.**

Length: over 65 feet
Life span: 10 years

THE **TWO DORSAL FINS** ARE POSITIONED **CLOSE** TO THE **TAIL.** THEY BOTH HAVE **FREE REAR TIPS.**

THERE ARE **THREE RIDGES** ALONG THE **SIDES** OF THE **BODY.**

THE **SKIN COLOR** IS **BLUISH-GREY,** FADING TO **WHITE** ON THE **BELLY.** THERE ARE **VERTICAL** AND **HORIZONTAL STRIPES** AND **WHITE SPOTS** ON THE **BACK.**

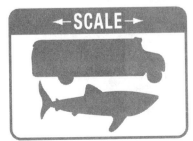

← SCALE →

WHERE THEY LIVE

WHALE SHARK

WHALE SHARKS **MIGRATE** PERIODICALLY, BUT NOT MUCH IS KNOWN ABOUT THEIR **MOVEMENTS.** IT HAS BEEN SAID THAT **MALES** MIGRATE **FURTHER** THAN FEMALES, AND THAT **FEMALES** ALWAYS **GO BACK** TO THEIR **NATIVE WATERS.**

WHALE SHARKS PROBABLY **MIGRATE** IN SEARCH OF **FOOD,** TO **MATE,** AND TO **GIVE BIRTH.**

WHALE SHARKS OFTEN FORM **HUGE SCHOOLS** OF OVER 100 INDIVIDUALS.

WHALE SHARKS SWIM NEAR THE **SURFACE** IN THE **WARM WATERS** OF THE **OPEN SEAS.** THIS IS WHERE THEIR MAIN SOURCE OF FOOD, **ZOOPLANKTON,** IS MOSTLY FOUND.

DESPITE THEIR **HUGE SIZE,** WHALE SHARKS ARE NOT A THREAT TO **PEOPLE.** THEY GENERALLY **IGNORE DIVERS** OR **SLOWLY MOVE AWAY** FROM THEM.

THE WHALE SHARK IS A **FILTER-FEEDER** AND EATS **ZOOPLANKTON**. IT LETS A **HUGE AMOUNT** OF **WATER** INTO ITS **MOUTH**, AND **PUSHES** IT **OUT** THROUGH ITS **GILL SLITS**. THE **GILLS** ARE **MODIFIED** TO **RETAIN** ALL THE **FOOD** AND **EXPEL** ONLY **WATER**.

ZOOPLANKTON IS MAINLY FOUND NEAR THE **SURFACE**. THAT IS WHERE WHALE SHARKS SWIM. THEY MOVE THEIR **HEADS** FROM **SIDE** TO **SIDE** WHILE SUCKING IN **WATER** AND **ZOOPLANKTON**, LIKE A **GIGANTIC VACUUM CLEANER**.

SOMETIMES, WHEN THEY **FEED**, WHALE SHARKS STAND **VERTICALLY** IN THE WATER WITH THEIR MOUTH **CLOSE** TO THE **SURFACE**.

WHALE SHARKS ARE **OVOVIVIPAROUS** AND GIVE **BIRTH** TO **300 PUPS!**

WHAT THEY EAT

Zooplankton

Small Bony Fish

Squid

Algae

SHARK Q&A

Yes, because sharks don't have a swim bladder like bony fish.

CAN SHARKS SWIM **BACKWARD?**

Sharks cannot swim backward or stop suddenly. This is because their fins aren't flexible like the ones of bony fish, but are very rigid.

CAN SHARKS STOP SWIMMING?

Many sharks can't. All sharks breathe by letting water inside their mouth and out from their gill slits. This is accomplished by swimming, because many sharks cannot suck the water in. But some sharks have spiracles that aid in the breathing process. These kinds of sharks don't have to always swim to breathe.

DO SHARKS SLEEP?

Scientists are not sure if sharks sleep like humans. Many species spend time resting at the bottom of the ocean, or in caves. Others are able to rest when swimming, in a kind of "auto-pilot" state.

In any case, sharks don't close their eyes and, although motionless, they seem to always be aware of their surroundings.

SHARKS' TAILS!

DEPENDING ON THE **SPECIES**, SHARKS HAVE DIFFERENT **SHAPED TAILS**. THE **TAIL** PLAYS AN **IMPORTANT ROLE** IN THE WAY SHARKS **SWIM** AND **HUNT**.

SLUGGISH SWIMMERS, LIKE THE **NURSE SHARK**, HAVE A **TAIL** WHICH **LACKS** THE **LOWER LOBE** ALMOST COMPLETELY. THEY SWIM, **UNDULATING** THEIR WHOLE **BODY**, VERY MUCH LIKE AN **EEL**.

SLUGGISH SHARKS FEED MOSTLY ON **SLOW-MOVING PREY**, LIKE **RAYS** AND **MOLLUSKS**. SWIMMING FAST IS NOT A **NECESSITY** FOR THEM.

TIGER SHARKS ARE **SCAVENGERS**, FEEDING ON **GARBAGE** AND **CARCASSES**. THEY DON'T SWIM FAST AND GENERALLY **CRUISE** THE **OCEANS** IN SEARCH OF FOOD. BUT TIGER SHARKS CAN **SUDDENLY ACCELERATE** AND **RAPIDLY TURN** TO CATCH **FAST-MOVING PREY**.

THE **LOWER LOBE** OF A TIGER SHARK TAIL IS MUCH **SMALLER** THAN THE **UPPER LOBE**. THIS TAIL CONFIGURATION **PROPELS** THE TIGER SHARK AT A **LOW SPEED** DURING **CRUISING**, BUT, WHEN NEEDED, ALLOWS FOR **QUICK BURSTS OF SPEED**.

THERE ARE MANY **FEATURES** THAT MAKE THE **SHORTFIN MAKO** THE **FASTER SWIMMER** OF ALL **SHARKS.** ONE OF THEM IS THE **SHAPE** OF ITS **TAIL.**

UNLIKE **NURSE SHARKS** AND **TIGER SHARKS' TAILS,** WHICH ARE **HETEROCERCAL,** SHORTFIN MAKOS TAILS ARE **HOMOCERCAL.** THIS MEANS THAT THE **TAIL LOBES** ARE **SYMMETRICAL,** WITH THE **LOWER LOBE** ALMOST AS **BIG** AS THE **UPPER LOBE.**

SHORTFIN MAKOS FEED ON **FAST-MOVING FISH** SUCH AS **TUNA, SWORDFISH,** AND OTHER **SHARKS.**

THRESHER SHARKS HAVE THE **LONGEST TAIL** OF ALL **SHARKS.** IT ACCOUNTS FOR ALMOST **50%** OF THEIR **TOTAL LENGTH.** THE **LOWER LOBE** IS **MUCH SMALLER** THAN THE **HUGE UPPER LOBE.**

THRESHER SHARKS USE THEIR **CAUDAL FIN** TO **SWIM FAST** IN **SHORT BURSTS,** BUT ALSO TO **HUNT.** WITH ITS TAIL, A THRESHER SHARK CAN **HERD** FISH INTO A **TIGHT SCHOOL.** THEN, IT **DIVES** INTO THE MIDDLE **GOBBLING** THE **FISH.** A THRESHER SHARK CAN ALSO **STUN** A **LARGE PREY** AND CATCH **SEABIRDS** WITH ITS TAIL.

SHARK BITEs!

19. WHAT SHOULD YOU DO WHEN YOU ARE WEARING A **GREEN BATHING SUIT** IN THE **RED SEA** AND YOU SEE A **BLUE SHARK?**

—SWIM AWAY AS **FAST** AS YOU CAN!

20. WHY WAS THE **HOSPITAL PATIENT NERVOUS?**

—BECAUSE HE HAD A **NURSE SHARK!**

21. DID YOU KNOW THAT THE **SHARK** FELL IN **LOVE** WITH THE **FISHERMAN?**

—YES, IT WAS **HOOKED** ON A FEELING!

Wrasses

JUST LIKE LAND ANIMALS, **SHARKS, BONY FISH,** AND **MARINE MAMMALS** ARE OFTEN PESTERED BY **PARASITES.** PARASITES LIVE UNDER THE **SCALES,** IN THE **GILLS,** OR ATTACH THEMSELVES TO THE **SKIN** OF AN **UNWILLING HOST.** THEY CAN CAUSE **IRRITATION** AND **ITCHINESS.** INFESTED **FISH** ARE OFTEN SEEN **RUBBING** THEMSELVES AGAINST **ROCKS** AND **CORALS,** TRYING TO FIND SOME RELIEF. **GREAT WHITES** AND **MAKOS** JUMP OUT OF THE WATER, **ATTEMPTING** TO **RID** THEMSELVES OF THEIR **PESTS.**

TO SOLVE THE **PARASITE PROBLEM,** BIG FISH, LIKE **SHARKS** AND **RAYS,** HAVE ENGAGED IN A **MUTUALISTIC RELATIONSHIP** WITH VERY **SMALL FISH,** GENERALLY **WRASSES,** OR SHRIMP. **MUTUALISTIC** MEANS THAT BOTH THE BIG FISH AND THE WRASSES **BENEFIT** FROM THE **RELATIONSHIP.**

SHARKS AND RAYS SWIM TO **SPECIFIC AREAS** OF THE **OCEAN** LOCATED IN THE **SHALLOW WATERS** OF **CORAL REEFS,** WHERE WRASSES LIVE. SCIENTISTS REFER TO THESE AREAS AS **"CLEANING STATIONS."** WRASSES ARE KNOWN TO **SWIM** IN A **DISTINCT WAY** TO **SIGNAL** THE **SHARKS** THAT THEY ARE **WILLING** TO **CLEAN** THEM. SHARKS **STAY STILL** WHILE WRASSES **RELIEVE** THEM OF **PARASITES** AND **DIRT.** SHARKS EVEN LET WRASSES **INSIDE** THEIR **MOUTHS** AND LET THEM **CLEAN** THEIR **TEETH** OF **FOOD LEFTOVERS.**

Cleaning stations are like a car wash for sharks!

WRASSES ARE KNOWN TO CLOSELY **INSPECT** AND **CLEAN** EVEN **SCUBA DIVERS,** IF THEY ARE WILLING TO STAY STILL **LONG ENOUGH!**

IN THE **CLEANING STATIONS,** SHARKS **DON'T PREY** ON WRASSES. THEIR **RELATIONSHIP** IS **BENEFICIAL** FOR THE SHARKS, BECAUSE IT **FREES** THEM OF **PARASITES.** IT'S ALSO **BENEFICIAL** FOR THE WRASSES THAT GET AN **EASY,** AND OFTEN **ABUNDANT, MEAL.** WRASSES DO SUCH A **GOOD JOB** THAT SOMETIMES **SHARKS** FORM A **LINE,** PATIENTLY WAITING FOR THEIR **TURN** TO BE **GROOMED.**

SWIMMING WITH SHARKS

Remoras

JUST LIKE WRASSES, **REMORAS** HAVE DEVELOPED A **RELATIONSHIP** WITH **SHARKS.** THEIR RELATIONSHIP IS CALLED **COMMENSALISM.** THIS MEANS THAT THE SHARK AND THE REMORA **SHARE** THE SAME **MEAL,** CAPTURED BY THE SHARK.

WHILE THE **RELATIONSHIP** BETWEEN **SHARKS** AND **WRASSES** IS **BENEFICIAL** FOR **BOTH PARTIES,** THE **RELATIONSHIP** BETWEEN **REMORAS** AND **SHARKS** IS BENEFICIAL **ONLY** FOR THE **REMORAS.** BUT **REMORAS** CANNOT BE CONSIDERED **PARASITES** BECAUSE THEY **DON'T HARM** THE SHARKS.

IN PLACE OF THE **DORSAL FIN**, REMORAS HAVE A **FLAT AREA** THAT CREATES **SUCTION** WHEN IN **CONTACT** WITH THE **SKIN** OF A **SHARK**. REMORAS CAN **ATTACH** AND **DETACH** THEMSELVES FROM THEIR **HOST** AT WILL.

REMORAS REAP **MANY BENEFITS** FROM THEIR **RELATIONSHIP** WITH **SHARKS**. THEY **GET FOOD** WITHOUT HAVING TO **HUNT** FOR IT. THEY GET **PROTECTION**, BECAUSE THE **PRESENCE** OF THE **SHARK** DETERS **ATTACKERS**. AND, STUCK TO THEIR HOST, THEY GET TO TRAVEL **GREAT DISTANCES** WITHOUT HAVING TO **SWIM**. FORTUNATELY FOR THE REMORAS, SHARKS DON'T SEEM TO **MIND** HAVING A FISH **GLUED** TO THEIR **BODIES**!

SOMETIMES REMORAS **ATTACH** THEMSELVES TO **SHIPS**. IN **ANCIENT GREECE** AND **ROME**, REMORAS WERE THOUGHT TO ACTUALLY **SLOW DOWN** THE SHIPS. IN FACT, THE WORD **REMORA** COMES FROM THE LATIN AND MEANS *"TO DELAY."*

SWIMMING WITH SHARKS

Pilot Fish

PILOT FISH, LIKE REMORAS, HAVE A **RELATIONSHIP** WITH **SHARKS** BASED ON **COMMENSALISM**. THIS MEANS THAT WHILE THE PILOT FISH GET **BENEFITS** FROM ITS ASSOCIATION WITH SHARKS, THE SHARK GETS NEITHER **BENEFITS** NOR **DISADVANTAGES**.

ONE OF THE **BENEFITS** FROM BEING **ASSOCIATED** WITH A **SHARK** IS THE **FREE FOOD**. PILOT FISH FEED ON **SCRAPS** AND **LEFTOVERS** OF THE SHARK'S **MEAL** AND DON'T HAVE TO **HUNT** FOR THEIR FOOD. THEY ALSO GET **PROTECTION** FROM **PREDATORS**, WHICH ARE **DETERRED** BY THE **PRESENCE** OF THE **SHARK**.

PILOT FISH **ACCOMPANY** SHARKS ON THEIR **TRAVELS**. THEY ARE OFTEN SEEN **PRECEDING** THE SHARK. FOR THIS REASON, PEOPLE THOUGHT THAT PILOT FISH WERE **GUIDING** (OR PILOTING) SHARKS TO **FOOD SOURCES** OR POSSIBLE **PREY**. BUT THIS TURNED OUT TO BE **UNTRUE**. SHARKS ARE ABLE TO **FIND** THEIR **PREY** WITH OR WITHOUT PILOT FISH.

SOMETIMES PILOT FISH **FOLLOW** A **SHIP**. ANCIENT EGYPTIANS HAD NOTED THIS **BEHAVIOR**. BACK THEN IT WAS BELIEVED THAT THE **SUN GOD RA** HAD **TWO SHIPS**, A **BIG ONE** FOR TRAVELING DURING THE **DAY** AND A **SMALL ONE** FOR TRAVELING AT **NIGHT**. BOTH **SHIPS** WERE **GUIDED** BY TWO **PILOT FISH** NAMED **ABTU** AND **ANT**.

PILOT FISH ACCOMPANY OTHER KINDS OF **MARINE ANIMALS** BESIDES SHARKS. THEY ARE SEEN WITH **RAYS, WHALES,** AND **TURTLES**. PILOT FISH ARE ALSO ABLE TO TAKE CARE OF THEMSELVES, **HUNTING** FOR **FOOD** WITHOUT HAVING TO **RELY** ON THEIR **TRAVEL COMPANIONS**.

PORT JACKSON SHARK

Heterodontus portusjacksoni

Order Herodontiformes (Bullhead Sharks)
Family Heterodontidae (Bullhead Sharks and Horn Sharks)

THE **FAMILY COMMON NAME** REFERS TO THE **PROTRUDING KNOBS** ON THE **BULLHEAD SHARKS' HEADS**, LIKE THE **HORNS** ON THE **HEAD** OF A **BULL**.

THE LATIN NAME **HETERODONTUS** COMES FROM GREEK WORDS, AND MEANS **"DIFFERENT TEETH."** IN FACT, **BULLHEAD SHARKS** HAVE **DIFFERENT** KINDS OF **TEETH** IN THEIR **MOUTHS**. THE **FRONT ONES** ARE **POINTY** FOR **GRABBING PREY**, WHILE THE **BACK ONES** ARE **FLAT** FOR **CRUSHING SHELLFISH**.

THE NAME **PORTUSJACKSONI** REFERS TO THE PLACE THESE SHARKS WERE **OBSERVED** FOR THE FIRST TIME. **PORT JACKSON** IS LOCATED IN **SYDNEY HARBOR**, AUSTRALIA.

THE **LIPS** ARE COVERED WITH **HARD CARTILAGE**, WHICH **PROTECTS** THE **MOUTH** AGAINST **PRICKLY SEA URCHINS**, THE PORT JACKSON SHARKS' **FAVORITE FOOD**.

THIS SHARK IS **YELLOWISH-GREY** WITH **SADDLE-LIKE BLOTCHES** ON ITS **BACK**.

← SCALE →

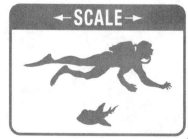

A PORT JACKSON SHARK **MALE** IS GENERALLY **TWO** AND **A HALF FEET** LONG. **FEMALES** ARE **BIGGER**, ALMOST **THREE FEET LONG**. WHEN THEY HATCH, **PUPS** ARE **TEN INCHES** LONG.

EACH OF THE **DORSAL FINS** IS PRECEDED BY A **BLUNT** AND **POISONOUS SPINE**. THE **SPINE** OF THE **PORT JACKSON SHARK PUPS** IS MUCH **SHARPER** THAN THAT OF AN ADULT. THE SPINE **PROTECTS** THIS SHARK AGAINST POSSIBLE **PREDATORS**.

PORT JACKSON SHARKS ARE **BOTTOM-DWELLERS** AND PREFER **ROCKY** OR **SEAGRASS BOTTOMS**.

THEY LIVE IN **WATERS** THAT ARE BETWEEN **THREE** AND **TEN** FEET DEEP.

WHERE THEY LIVE

Length: 2.5 feet
Width: 3 feet

PORT JACKSON SHARK

PORT JACKSON SHARK ADULTS HAVE **FLAT TEETH** TO **CRUSH** THE SHELLS OF **SHELLFISH** AND **SEA URCHINS**, WHICH THEY SWALLOW WHOLE. AFTER HAVING **DIGESTED** THE **SOFT PARTS**, THE PORT JACKSON SHARKS **VOMIT** THE **HARD PARTS**.

PORT JACKSON SHARK **JUVENILES** HAVE **POINTY TEETH** BECAUSE THEY FEED MOSTLY ON **WORMS** THAT **HIDE** IN THE **SAND**. TO CATCH THEM, THE YOUNG SHARKS **SUCK** SAND INTO THEIR **MOUTHS**, SWALLOW THE **WORMS**, AND **EXPEL** THE SAND THROUGH THEIR **GILL SLITS**.

THE PORT JACKSON SHARK IS NOT CONSIDERED **DANGEROUS**, BUT, IF DISTURBED, IT CAN **BITE** OR IT CAN **STING** WITH ITS **SPINES**. IT HAS BEEN REPORTED THAT, IF NOT MADE TO FEEL **THREATENED**, THE PORT JACKSON SHARK LET DIVERS **PET** IT!

Shark Tales: Fossils of bullhead sharks have been found that are over 200 million years old!

EACH YEAR, PORT JACKSON SHARKS RETURN TO THE SAME **BREEDING PLACES**, SOMETIMES AFTER SWIMMING FOR OVER **500 MILES**! THESE SHARKS ARE **OVIPAROUS** AND LAY **EGGS**. THE EGGS ARE IN THE SHAPE OF A **SCREW**. THE **SHELL** IS **BLACK** AND ABOUT **SIX INCHES** LONG. ONCE LAID, THE EGG SHELLS ARE **SOFT** AND THE PORT JACKSON SHARK FEMALE **STUFFS** THEM INTO **ROCK CREVICES**. SOON, THE SHELLS **HARDEN UP** INSIDE THE CREVICE, AND THE EGGS BECOME **IMPOSSIBLE** TO **DISLODGE**. IN THIS WAY, THE EGGS ARE **PROTECTED** FROM **PREDATORS**.

OTHER SHARKS IN THIS FAMILY, LIKE THE **CRESTED BULLHEAD SHARK**, LAY **TENDRILED EGGS**. THE TENDRILS ARE **SIX FEET LONG**! TO **HIDE** THEM FROM **PREDATORS**, THESE SHARKS TIE THE EGGS BY THEIR TENDRILS TO UNDERWATER **CORALS** OR **ROCKS**

MOST SHARKS NEED TO **SWIM** IN ORDER TO **BREATHE**. WHEN THEY SWIM, THEY KEEP THEIR **MOUTH** OPEN, LETTING IN **WATER**. THE WATER GOES FROM THE MOUTH TO THE **GILLS,** LOCATED ON BOTH **SIDES** OF THE **HEAD**. THE GILLS **EXTRACT OXYGEN** FROM THE WATER. THEN, THE WATER IS **PUSHED OUT** FROM THE **GILL SLITS**.

SOME SHARKS ARE ABLE TO BREATHE **WITHOUT** HAVING TO **SWIM**. THE **PORT JACKSON SHARK** CAN **SUCK IN** WATER FROM ITS **FIRST GILL SLIT** AND **EXPEL** IT FROM THE **OTHER SLITS**. IN THIS WAY, THIS SHARK CAN REMAIN **MOTIONLESS** ON THE OCEAN FLOOR, WITHOUT HAVING TO CONTINUOUSLY SWIM.

PORT JACKSON SHARKS ARE **NOCTURNAL**. DURING THE **DAY,** THEY CONGREGATE IN **GROUPS** OF ABOUT **15 INDIVIDUALS** AND **REST** TOGETHER, **HIDING** IN **CAVES**.

WHAT THEY EAT

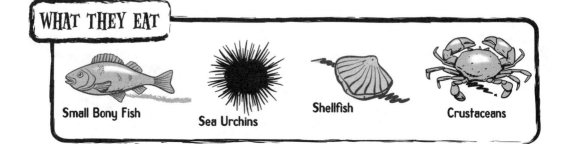

Small Bony Fish

Sea Urchins

Shellfish

Crustaceans

WHICH IS THE FASTEST SHARK?

The fastest shark is the shortfin mako, which can swim at bursts of 20 miles per hour.

HOW LONG CAN SHARKS LIVE?

Many species live an average of 30 years, but some sharks are known to live up to 100! Sharks kept in captivity live longer.

WHAT IS A FEEDING FRENZY?

Some sharks, like the blacktip shark, become extremely excited in the presence of food. Their excitement can reach such a feverish pitch that sharks might end up attacking, injuring, and even killing and eating each other!

WHICH IS THE SHARKS' FINEST SENSE?

It's the sense of smell, because a large part of the shark brain is dedicated to interpreting signals coming from the nostrils.

WHEN SHARKS ATTACK!

Sharks don't hunt for humans as people are not part of their natural diet. But sharks can attack people, and sometimes these attacks result in fatalities. ISAF, the International Shark Attack File, reports that there are an average of 70 to 100 non-provoked shark attacks every year worldwide. Between 5 to 15 of these attacks are fatal. Non-provoked attacks mean that the victim had not intentionally provoked the shark. But the shark might have a different opinion!

It has been reported that many shark attacks happen because the victim wasn't aware that he or she was intruding upon the shark's personal space. Other attacks happen because the victim wasn't aware of the warning signs the shark had sent out. These signs are comparable to a dog showing its teeth and growling right before attacking. A shark's warning signs include arching its back, lowering its tail and pectoral fins, and swimming in circles.

BELIEVE IT OR NOT, SOME DIVERS **PROVOKE SHARKS** INTO **ATTACKING THEM!**

THERE I WAS, MINDING MY OWN BUSINESS...

PERSONAL SPACE!

Sharks are extremely curious. The best way for a shark to figure out what something is, other than smelling it, is biting it. Sharks often don't like the taste of people, and quickly release their victim. But even a small exploratory bite can be very painful for a person.

ONLY **30%** OF **SHARK SPECIES** HAVE BEEN **INVOLVED** IN **ATTACKS** ON **HUMANS.**

A shark attack is an extremely stressful and painful experience for the victims and their families. But only a yearly average of 80 people worldwide are attacked by sharks. Here are some comparisons to put shark attacks in perspective. The numbers refer to a yearly average and are limited to occurrences in the United States.

IN THE UNITED STATES...

...100 people die struck by lightning.

...100 people die from a reaction to bee stings.

...550 people die in bicycle accidents.

...42,000 people die in car crashes.

...750 people drown.

WORLDWIDE...an average of 10 people die of a shark attack.

WHEN SHARKS ATTACK!

10 THINGS TO DO TO AVOID A SHARK ATTACK:

1 DON'T SWIM AT NIGHT!

Many sharks are more active at night and early in the morning than during the day. Also, at night, it's more difficult for you to be aware of the presence of sharks.

2 DON'T SWIM IN MURKY WATERS!

Just like at night time, it's hard to be aware of the presence of a shark in dirty waters.

3 DON'T CARRY DEAD FISH!

Sharks' nostrils can detect the smell of dead fish from far away. So, try to avoid going spear-fishing.

4 DON'T SWIM IF YOU ARE BLEEDING!

Sharks can sense blood from far away and are attracted to it.

5 DON'T SWIM IN SHARKS' FAVORITE PLACES!

Avoid swimming in channels, steep drop-offs, and harbor entrances, because sharks like to swim in these places.

6 DON'T WEAR JEWELRY!

Sharks are attracted to shimmering things, such as jewelry, since they are similar to the iridescence of fish scales.

7 DON'T SWIM WITH DOLPHINS!

Avoid swimming if you see dolphins and seabirds gathering in one spot. This means that they are feeding on a school of fish, the same prey sharks like. Keep in mind that dolphins don't chase away sharks. Actually, sharks prey on dolphins.

8 DON'T SWIM NEAR GARBAGE!

Stay away from places where there's garbage. Many sharks are opportunistic hunters and garbage offers them plenty of leftovers.

9 DON'T SWIM ALONE!

Don't swim alone far away from shore.

10 DON'T BUG THE SHARKS!

And, of course, if you see a shark, don't disturb it!

WHEN SHARKS ATTACK!

WHAT TO DO IF YOU ARE SWIMMING AND SEE A SHARK:

1 DON'T PANIC!

Sharks are attracted to erratic movements because they are a signal that the potential victim is in distress.

2 SWIM TO SHORE!

Swim to the closest place that is out of the water.

3 SWIM RHYTHMICALLY!

Erratic movements are typical of a fish in distress. This is a shark's perfect prey because injured animals are easy to catch. So, keep swimming with rhythmical movements.

4 KEEP AN EYE ON THE SHARK!

Try to always be aware of where the shark is in relation to you.

5 BE PREPARED TO FIGHT!

If the shark is persistent, be prepared to hit it. The best places are its eyes, gills, and snout.

WHAT TO DO IF YOU SEE SOMEONE BITTEN BY A SHARK:

1 ACT QUICKLY!

Act as quickly as possible. It can save the victim's life!

2 BRING VICTIM TO SHORE!

Bring the victim out of the water to a safe place!

3 STOP THE BLEEDING!

Apply pressure to the wound to stop the bleeding.

100

4 GET HELP!

Call the emergency ward or 911.

5 STAY WITH THE VICTIM!

Keep the victim warm and still while waiting for the emergency relief to arrive.

BATOIDS ARE FISH **RELATED** TO **SHARKS** BECAUSE THEY BOTH BELONG TO THE SAME **CLASS**. THE CLASS IS CALLED **CHONDRICHTHYES**. THESE ARE **FISH** WITH A **SKELETON** MADE OF **CARTILAGE**.

BATOIDS INCLUDE **RAYS, SKATES, STINGRAYS, CHIMAERAS, GUITARFISH,** AND **SAWFISH**.

MANY OF THESE FISH HAVE A **FLAT BODY** SIMILAR TO THAT OF **ANGELSHARKS**. THE **DIFFERENCE** BETWEEN THESE FISH IS THAT THE **WINGS** OF THE **ANGELSHARKS** AREN'T ATTACHED TO THE **HEAD**.

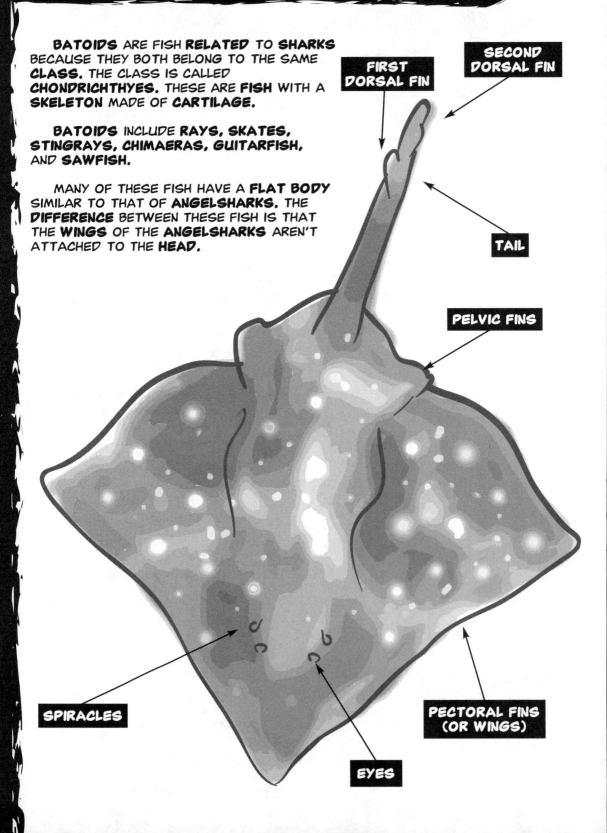

FIRST DORSAL FIN

SECOND DORSAL FIN

TAIL

PELVIC FINS

SPIRACLES

PECTORAL FINS (OR WINGS)

EYES

JUST LIKE SHARKS, **RAYS** AND **SKATES** HAVE **FIVE GILL SLITS**. THEY ARE POSITIONED **UNDER** THE **BODY**. THERE'S ONLY **ONE FAMILY** OF RAYS, CALLED **HEXATRYGONIDAE**, THAT HAVE **SIX GILL SLITS**.

NOSTRILS

MOUTH

GILL SLITS

CLOACA

BATOIDS ARE FOUND IN EVERY **OCEAN** AND **SEA**, SOMETIMES EVEN IN **BRACKISH WATERS**. THEY LIVE ON **SANDY** OR **MUDDY SEAFLOORS**, FEEDING ON **MOLLUSKS, SMALL FISH, WORMS**, AND **CRUSTACEANS**, LIKE CRABS, LOBSTERS, AND SHRIMP. ALL BATOIDS ARE **CARNIVOROUS**.

BATOIDS DON'T HAVE ANY **ANAL FINS**.

BATOIDS **DESCEND** FROM **SHARKS**.

BATOIDS HAVE **EYES** AND **SPIRACLES** ON **TOP** OF THEIR **HEADS**, WHILE THE **GILL SLITS** ARE **UNDER** THEIR **BODIES**. THEY OFTEN **BURY** THEMSELVES IN THE **SAND** AND CAN'T **BREATHE** THROUGH THEIR **GILL SLITS**. SO, THEY USE THEIR **SPIRACLES** INSTEAD.

THERE ARE A LOT MORE **RAY** AND **SKATE SPECIES** (OVER 550) THAN THERE ARE **SHARKS**. BATOID SPECIES ARE ARRANGED IN ABOUT **18 FAMILIES**.

Shark Tales: In 1608, when Captain John Smith and his crew were exploring the Rappahannock River, John was stung by a stingray on his arm. The pain was intense, and his arm turned blue and swelled. John Smith believed he was going to die and chose a place for his burial. Eventually, John survived the painful experience and ended up having the stingray that hurt him for dinner! The place in which he got stung is still called Stingray Point.

CLEARNOSE SKATE

Raja eglanteria

THE **CLEARNOSE SKATE** IS THE **MOST COMMON** SKATE ON THE **EASTERN COAST** OF THE **UNITED STATES.**

CLEARNOSE SKATES ARE KNOWN AS **BRIER SKATES** BECAUSE OF THE **THORNS** ON THEIR **BACKS.** BRIERS ARE **PRICKLY PLANTS.**

THE **TWO LIGHT BROWN PATCHES** ON THE **SNOUT** OF THIS SKATE INSPIRED THE NAME **"CLEARNOSE."**

SKATES SWIM **FLAPPING** THEIR **WINGS,** GLIDING THROUGH THE WATER.

CLEARNOSE SKATES ARE **OVIPAROUS.** THE **EGGS** ARE EQUIPPED WITH **HORNS** FOR PROTECTION, AND ARE **THREE INCHES LONG.**

Length: 2.5 feet

← SCALE →

WHERE THEY LIVE

Clearnose skates migrate to warmer waters during the winter.

THE CLEARNOSE SKATE HAS **ONE ROW** OF **THORNS** ALONG ITS **SPINE.** THERE ARE OVER **15 THORNS** ALONG ITS **BACK.** MORE **THORN PATCHES** ARE FOUND AROUND THE **EYES, SHOULDERS,** AND **TAIL.**

THE CLEARNOSE SKATE IS **DARK BROWN** WITH **BLACK SPOTS** AND **BARS.**

WHAT THEY EAT

Small Bony Fish

Cephalopods like Squid

Crustaceans

Worms

Bivalves

SOUTHERN STINGRAY

Dasyatis americana

SOUTHERN STINGRAYS ARE KNOWN TO MEET UP WITH **WRASSES**, SMALL FISH, IN **SPECIFIC AREAS** OF **OCEANS** MARINE BIOLOGISTS CALL **CLEANING STATIONS**. WHILE THE STINGRAYS STAY STILL, WRASSES **LOOK FOR**, AND **EAT**, THE **PARASITES** THAT **INFEST** THEIR BODY.

SOUTHERN STINGRAYS REPRODUCE THROUGH **OVOVIVIPARITY**. THIS MEANS THAT DURING THE **GESTATION PERIOD**, THE **EMBRYOS** ARE NOT CONNECTED TO THEIR **MOTHER** THROUGH A **PLACENTA**. IT ALSO MEANS THAT THE EMBRYOS ARE **DELIVERED ALIVE** BY THE MOTHER, NOT ENCASED IN EGGSHELLS.

DURING THE GESTATION PERIOD, THE EMBRYOS FEED ON A **WHITE SUBSTANCE** SECRETED BY THE MOTHER DIRECTLY INTO ITS **UTERUS**. THIS IS CALLED **UTERINE MILK**.

A SOUTHERN STINGRAY CAN DELIVER UP TO **TEN PUPS**.

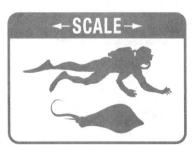

←SCALE→

STINGRAYS HAVE A **WHIP-LIKE TAIL** AND **NO FINS.** DEPENDING ON THE SPECIES, THE TAIL BEARS UP TO **EIGHT STINGERS** TO BE USED IN SELF-DEFENSE. EACH **EIGHT-INCH LONG STINGER** IS INSIDE A **SHEATH** OF **SKIN,** WHICH IS **PUSHED BACK** DURING AN **ATTACK.** THE BARBED EDGES MAKE THE STINGER **HARD** AND **PAINFUL** TO **EXTRACT.** STINGRAYS CAN **RE-GROW** THEIR STINGERS.

STINGERS DELIVER **POISON.** UNLESS A **VITAL ORGAN** IS **STUNG,** STINGRAY POISON ISN'T **DEADLY,** BUT CAUSES **SEVERE PAIN** AND **SWELLING.**

STINGRAYS ARE **DOCILE** ANIMALS, BUT ARE OFTEN **BURIED** IN **SAND,** AS THIS IS ONE OF THEIR **HUNTING TECHNIQUES.** FOR THIS REASON IT'S VERY COMMON TO **STEP** ON THEM, AND BE **STUNG** IN **RETURN.**

PEOPLE WHO GET STUNG SHOULD RECEIVE **IMMEDIATE MEDICAL ATTENTION.** THE STINGER SHOULD BE **REMOVED** AND THE **INFECTION TREATED.** THE INTENSE PAIN CAN BE ALLEVIATED BY **IMMERSING** THE **WOUND** IN **HOT WATER.**

STINGER

Closeup of a stingray's tail.

SOUTHERN STINGRAYS **HIDE** IN THE **SANDY BOTTOMS** OF **SHALLOW WATERS.** THEY ARE OFTEN FOUND IN **ESTUARIES,** TOO.

THE **SOUTHERN STINGRAY'S BODY** IS IN THE SHAPE OF A **DIAMOND.** THE **WIDTH** IS ABOUT **FIVE FEET,** WHILE THE **LENGTH** IS **THREE** AND A **HALF FEET.** IT CAN **WEIGH** UP TO **300 POUNDS!**

Shark Tales: The southern stingray tail is two times the length of its body, or seven feet long!

WHAT THEY EAT

Mollusks
like clams

Crustaceans
like Crabs and Shrimp

WHERE THEY LIVE

Length: 3.5 feet
Weight: 300 lbs.

EAGLE RAY

Myliobatis freminvillii

AN **EAGLE RAY** FLIES THROUGH THE **WATER** FLAPPING ITS **BROAD WINGS**, JUST LIKE AN **EAGLE**, AS THE NAME SUGGESTS. EAGLE RAYS ARE EXTREMELY **GRACEFUL SWIMMERS**, BUT VERY **STRONG**, AND CAN SWIM FOR **VERY LONG DISTANCES**.

THE **TAIL** OF THE EAGLE RAY LOOKS LIKE A **WHIP**. AT THE **END** OF THE **TAIL** THERE'S A BARBED STINGER. THE **STINGER** IS HIGHLY **POISONOUS**.

THESE RAYS LIVE ALONG THE **COASTS** IN **SHALLOW WATERS**, UP TO **DEPTHS** OF **100 FEET**. THEY PREFER SAND OR **MUDDY BOTTOMS** AND ARE OFTEN FOUND **NEAR ESTUARIES**. THEY ARE GENERALLY SEEN GLIDING OVER THE **SEA FLOOR**, LOOKING FOR PREY.

EAGLE RAYS CAN **JUMP OUT** OF THE **WATER**.

WHERE THEY LIVE

Eagle rays are suspected to move to warmer waters during the winter.

Shark Tales: Ancestors of the eagle rays evolved at the end of the Cretaceous period, 100 million years ago, before the dinosaurs became extinct.

SOME SPECIES BELONGING TO THE **MYLIOBATIDAE FAMILY** CAN BE **8 FEET** WIDE AND WEIGH **850 POUNDS!** THE EAGLE RAY IS NOT AS BIG, MEASURING ONLY **3 FEET.**

WHAT THEY EAT

Mollusks like Clams

Crustaceans

THE **COLOR** OF THE **SKIN** VARIES FROM **BROWN** TO **GREY.** THE **BELLY** IS **WHITE.** THE **TEETH** ARE **GREEN.**

ALL **RAYS'** **PECTORAL FINS** ARE SHAPED LIKE **WINGS,** BUT THOSE OF THE **EAGLE RAY** ARE **VERY POINTY.**

THERE'S A **POINTED BEAK** ON THE SNOUT. WITH IT, THE EAGLE RAY DIGS UP **CLAMS.** THEN, IT CRUSHES THEM WITH ITS **POWERFUL TEETH.**

← SCALE →

ROUND STINGRAY

Urolophus or Urobatis halleri

ROUND STINGRAYS BURY THEMSELVES IN THE SAND OR MUD OF THE SEAFLOOR. FROM THIS HIDING POINT, THEY AWAIT FOR PREY. THEY OBSERVE THE SURROUNDING AREA WITH THEIR EYES, CONVENIENTLY POSITIONED ON TOP OF THEIR HEAD.

ANOTHER ROUND STINGRAY'S HUNTING TECHNIQUE CONSISTS OF FLAPPING ITS WINGS ON A SANDY BOTTOM. THE SAND IS SWEPT AWAY TO REVEAL BURIED PREY SUCH AS CRABS AND WORMS.

ROUND STINGRAYS ARE OVOVIVIPAROUS AND GIVE BIRTH AFTER A FOUR MONTH GESTATION PERIOD. THE PUP'S STINGER IS BENDABLE AND COVERED IN SKIN. THIS

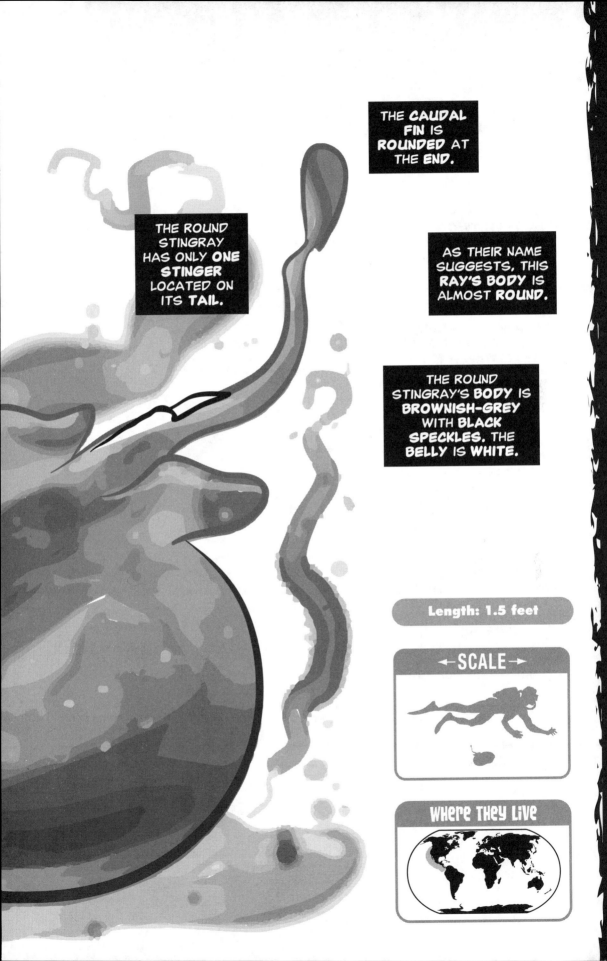

THE **CAUDAL FIN** IS **ROUNDED** AT THE **END.**

THE ROUND STINGRAY HAS ONLY **ONE STINGER** LOCATED ON ITS **TAIL.**

AS THEIR NAME SUGGESTS, THIS **RAY'S BODY** IS ALMOST **ROUND.**

THE ROUND STINGRAY'S **BODY** IS **BROWNISH-GREY** WITH **BLACK SPECKLES.** THE **BELLY** IS **WHITE.**

Length: 1.5 feet

←SCALE→

WHERE THEY LIVE

GIANT DEVIL RAY

Manta birostris

THE LATIN NAME **BIROSTRIS** MEANS **"WITH TWO HORNS."** IT REFERS TO THE **PROTRUDING CEPHALITIC FINS**, OR **LOBES**, ON THE RAY'S HEAD. THEY LOOK LIKE **HORNS** AND INSPIRED THE COMMON NAME, **DEVIL RAY**.

THE AVERAGE **GIANT DEVIL RAY** MEASURES **23 FEET** FROM **WING TIP** TO **WING TIP!** THEY ARE THE **BIGGEST RAYS** IN THE **WORLD**.

GIANT DEVIL RAYS SWIM IN **LARGE GROUPS.** THEY OFTEN **JUMP** TOGETHER CLEAR OUT OF THE **WATER.** THEIR JUMPS CAN BE **SIX FEET HIGH!** SCIENTISTS DON'T KNOW THE **MEANING** OF THIS **BEHAVIOR.** JUMPING COULD BE A **DISPLAY** OF **COURTSHIP** BECAUSE IT SEEMS TO HAPPEN IN SPECIFIC SEASONS, **SPRING** AND **FALL.** IT COULD BE THAT THESE RAYS ARE SIMPLY TRYING TO GET SOME **RELIEF** FROM THE **PARASITES** THAT PESTER THEM. BUT MAYBE THEY ARE SIMPLY **PLAYING.**

WHEN A GIANT DEVIL RAY JUMPS OUT OF THE WATER, IT CAN LAND **HEAD** OR **TAIL FIRST,** OR IT CAN EVEN **SOMERSAULT!**

THE **WINGS** ARE **TRIANGULAR** AND **POINTY.**

A **PUP** CAN **WEIGH** OVER **20 POUNDS** AT **BIRTH.**

THERE'S **NO STINGER** ON THE **WHIP-LIKE TAIL.**

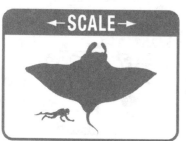
← SCALE →

WHERE THEY LIVE

THE GIANT DEVIL RAY KEEPS ITS **CEPHALITIC FINS** CLOSE TO ITS MOUTH. BUT WHEN IT'S **FEEDING,** THE FINS **UNFURL** TO **CREATE** A **CHANNEL** IN WHICH THE WATER **INESCAPABLY DRIVES FOOD** INTO THE **MOUTH.** THE **GILL RAKERS** SEPARATE THE **FOOD** FROM THE **WATER.**

UNLIKE THE OTHER RAYS, THE GIANT DEVIL RAYS **SWIM** JUST **UNDER** THE **SURFACE** OF THE **WATER,** AND THEY ARE NOT **BOTTOM-DWELLERS.** THE GIANT DEVIL RAY **BREATHES** MOSTLY **THROUGH** ITS **GILLS,** NOT ITS **SPIRACLES.** FOR THIS REASON, ITS **SPIRACLES** ARE **SMALL.**

WHAT THEY EAT

Small Bony Fish

Crustaceans

Zooplankton

THE **TWO CEPHALITIC FINS** ARE AN **EXTENSION** OF THE **PECTORAL FINS.**

THE COLOR OF THE **SKIN** IS **BLACK** OR **DARK BROWN** ON TOP. THE **BELLY** IS **WHITE.** SOMETIMES THERE ARE **WHITE BLOTCHES** ON THE **BACK** AND **BLACK BLOTCHES** ON THE **BELLY.** THESE **MARKINGS** ARE **UNIQUE** TO EACH **INDIVIDUAL.**

Shark Tales: A legend from the State of Yap, of the Federates States of Micronesia, narrates that giant devil rays can wrap themselves around people. Then, they drag their victims into the abyss, drowning them. But this is not true. Giant devil rays are extremely docile although they command respect for their huge size.

LONG-NOSED CHIMAERA

Harriotta raleighana

IN GREEK MYTHOLOGY, **CHIMAERA** WAS A **FIRE-BREATHING, FLYING MONSTER.** ITS **BODY** WAS MADE UP OF **THREE DIFFERENT ANIMALS.** THE **FRONT PART** WAS THAT OF A **LION,** THE **HIND** PART WAS THAT OF A **GOAT,** AND IT HAD A **SNAKE** FOR THE **TAIL.** CHIMAERA WAS KILLED BY THE GREEK HERO **BELLEROPHON** WHILE RIDING **PEGASUS,** THE **WINGED HORSE.**

JUST AS THE **MYTHOLOGICAL CHIMAERA** WAS MADE UP OF DIFFERENT ANIMALS, THE **CHIMAERA FISH** SEEMS TO HAVE **SHARKS, RAYS,** AND **BONY FISH FEATURES.** CHIMAERAS HAVE A **SKELETON** MADE OF **CARTILAGE,** LIKE **SHARKS** AND **RAYS.** CHIMAERAS' **GILLS** ARE COVERED BY A **FLAP,** LIKE **BONY FISH.** CHIMAERAS HAVE **TONGUES,** LIKE **SHARKS,** BUT UNLIKE **RAYS,** WHICH LACK THIS **FEATURE.**

AS THE **COMMON NAME** SUGGESTS, THE **LONG-NOSED CHIMAERAS** HAVE A **LONG SNOUT.** THE **SNOUT** IS **SOFT, WIDE** IN THE **MIDDLE,** AND END WITH A **POINT.**

Length: 4 feet

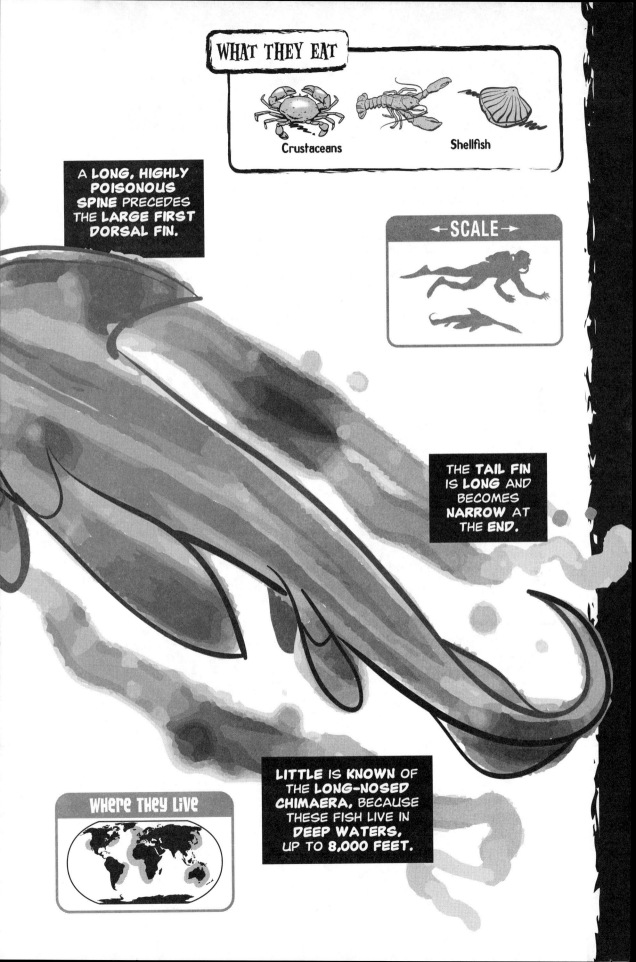

WHAT THEY EAT

Crustaceans   Shellfish

A **LONG, HIGHLY POISONOUS SPINE** PRECEDES THE **LARGE FIRST DORSAL FIN.**

← SCALE →

THE **TAIL FIN** IS **LONG** AND BECOMES **NARROW** AT THE **END.**

WHERE THEY LIVE

LITTLE IS KNOWN OF THE **LONG-NOSED CHIMAERA,** BECAUSE THESE FISH LIVE IN **DEEP WATERS,** UP TO **8,000 FEET.**

ELECTRIC RAY

Torpedo nobiliana

THE LATIN NAME **TORPEDO** COMES FROM A GREEK WORD THAT MEANS "**TORPID**," OR "**NUMB**." IT REFERS TO THE ABILITY OF THIS **RAY** TO **SHOCK** ITS **VICTIM** WITH **ELECTRICITY**.

THE **ELECTRIC RAY'S SHOCK** IS **220 VOLTS** AND IT'S STRONG ENOUGH TO **KNOCK** A **MAN DOWN** OR TO **LIGHT** A **BULB!** ELECTRIC RAYS USE THEIR **ELECTRICITY** AS A **SELF-DEFENSE MECHANISM** AND FOR **HUNTING**.

DESPITE BEING **SLUGGISH ANIMALS**, ELECTRIC RAYS CAN CAPTURE **FAST-SWIMMING FISH**. THEY **AMBUSH** THEIR VICTIMS **HIDING** IN THE **SAND**. WHEN ONE SWIMS BY, THE ELECTRIC RAY **BLASTS** IT WITH **ELECTRICITY** BY **WRAPPING** ITS **WINGS** AROUND IT. THEN, THE **STUNNED PREY** IS EATEN.

THE SKIN COLOR IS **BROWN** OR **DARK PURPLE**. THE BELLY IS **WHITE**.

WHAT THEY EAT

Small Bony Fish

THE ELECTRIC RAY CAN BLAST **ELECTRICITY** FOR QUITE SOME **TIME**. BUT THE **BLASTS** GET **WEAKER** AND **WEAKER**. THEY COME BACK TO THEIR **FULL POTENCY** AFTER THE ELECTRIC RAY SPENDS SOME TIME **RESTING**.

← SCALE →

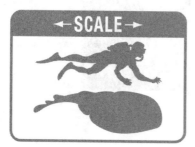

WHERE THEY LIVE

ELECTRIC RAY **JUVENILES** LIVE IN **SHALLOW WATERS** UP TO **1,000 FEET DEEP**. **ADULTS** CAN **SWIM** FOR **GREAT DISTANCES**.

THE **ABILITY** TO PRODUCE **ELECTRICITY** IS CALLED **ELECTROGENESIS**. THE **ORGANS** THAT PRODUCE ELECTRICITY ARE LOCATED IN THE **PECTORAL FINS**.

THE **BODY** OF THE ELECTRIC RAY IS **ROUND, UP** TO **SIX FEET WIDE**. THERE ARE **TWO DORSAL FINS** ON THE **TAIL**. THE **TAIL ENDS** IN A **PADDLE-LIKE SHAPE**.

Shark Tales: Ancient Romans believed that electric rays could cure gout, a painful inflammation of the joints. Patients had to stand on top of an electric ray, in the water, until their foot and leg were numbed by the electric shocks. This treatment supposedly stopped the pain of gout from coming back.

SPOTTED GUITARFISH

Rhinobatos lentiginosus

THE LATIN WORD **RHINOBATOS** MEANS **"NOSED RAY."** UNLIKE MOST RAYS, THE **SPOTTED GUITARFISH** HAS A **PROTRUDING SNOUT.** THE WORD **LENTIGINOSUS** MEANS **"FRECKLED"** AND REFERS TO THE **SPOTS** ON THE **BACK.**

THE **SHAPE** OF THE **BODY** INSPIRED THE ENGLISH COMMON NAME **GUITARFISH.** IN OTHER COUNTRIES, THE SHAPE OF THE GUITARFISH INSPIRED DIFFERENT COMMON NAMES, SUCH AS **VIOLA, VIOLIN, FIDDLE,** AND **BANJO.**

THERE ARE **THORNY DENTICLES** ON THE **SNOUT.**

SPOTTED GUITARFISH LIVE ON THE **SEA FLOOR,** BURIED IN **SANDY** OR **MUDDY BOTTOMS,** AT NO MORE THAN **100 FEET DEEP.**

← SCALE →

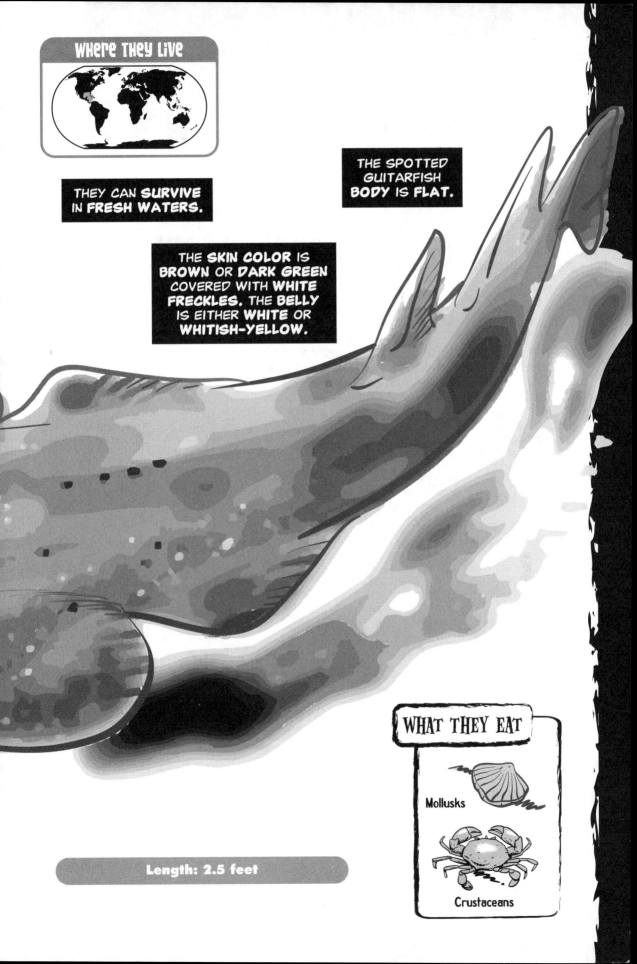

WHERE THEY LIVE

THEY CAN **SURVIVE** IN **FRESH WATERS.**

THE SPOTTED GUITARFISH **BODY IS FLAT.**

THE **SKIN COLOR** IS **BROWN** OR **DARK GREEN** COVERED WITH **WHITE FRECKLES.** THE **BELLY** IS EITHER **WHITE** OR **WHITISH-YELLOW.**

Length: 2.5 feet

WHAT THEY EAT

Mollusks

Crustaceans

SMALLTOOTH SAWFISH

Pristis pectinata

THE WORD **PRISTIS** COMES FROM THE GREEK AND MEANS **"SAW."** THIS SPECIES IS CALLED **SMALLTOOTH** BECAUSE THE **TEETH** ON THE **SNOUT** ARE **SMALLER** THAN THOSE ON OTHER SPECIES OF **SAWFISH.**

SHARKS CAN **REPLACE** THEIR **TEETH** THROUGHOUT THEIR LIVES BECAUSE THEIR TEETH ARE **LOOSELY ATTACHED** TO THE **JAWS.** UNLIKE SHARKS, **SAWFISH TEETH** ARE **EMBEDDED** IN THE **CARTILAGE** OF THE **SNOUT** AND ARE **NOT REPLACEABLE.** EVENTUALLY, THEY BECOME **BLUNT** WITH USAGE.

SAWFISH USE THEIR **TOOTHED SNOUT** TO CAPTURE **PREY.** THEY HAVE **TWO HUNTING TECHNIQUES.**

IN THE FIRST ONE, SAWFISH **SWING** THEIR **HEAD** FROM **SIDE** TO **SIDE** AND **IMPALE** THEIR **PREY** WITH THEIR **TOOTHED SNOUT.** THEY **DETACH** THE **PREY** BY **SCRAPING** THEIR SNOUT AGAINST THE **SEAFLOOR.** THEN, THEY **EAT** IT.

THE SECOND **HUNTING TECHNIQUE** CONSISTS OF **SCOURING** SANDY OR MUDDY BOTTOMS WITH THEIR SNOUT. IN THIS WAY, THEY UNCOVER AND EAT **BURIED WORMS** AND **CRUSTACEANS.**

Length: 20 feet

Shark Tales: Sawfish litters can yield over 20 pups each. The pups' snouts and teeth are soft, so the mother doesn't get hurt giving birth. After birth, the pups' snouts and teeth harden up.

SAWFISH CAN SURVIVE IN **FRESH WATERS.** IN THE **UNITED STATES,** SAWFISH ARE FOUND IN THE **MISSISSIPPI, RED RIVER,** AND RIVERS OF **NORTH CAROLINA.**

←SCALE→

THE AVERAGE SAWFISH IS ABOUT **20 FEET LONG.** THE **SNOUT** IS **FIVE FEET** LONG OR **25%** OR THE **TOTAL LENGTH.**

WHERE THEY LIVE

WHAT THEY EAT

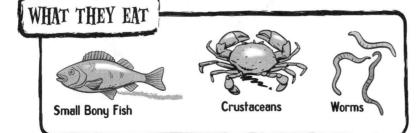

Small Bony Fish   Crustaceans   Worms

SHARK ATTACKERS!

The general fish population is decreasing because of over-fishing, habitat destruction, and pollution. With the decline of fish used for human consumption, fisheries are becoming more interested in exploiting sharks for this same reason.

In Asia, the demand for shark fins is very high because they are used to prepare an Oriental delicacy, shark fin soup. Sharks are fished only for their fins. The mutilated sharks are dumped back into the ocean to die.

Many sharks are simply fished for sport. Some waters are protected against this type of fishing, but sharks can travel very long distances daily. This means that, when they enter unprotected waters, they can be legally fished for sport. Sharks fished for this reason are often dumped.

In many countries, sharks are caught for their jaws, teeth, and skin. It has been reported that the jaw of a great white is valued at $10,000 in South Africa. This lucrative and illegal trading is mindless of the fact that many sharks are listed as an endangered and protected species.

Sharks shouldn't be considered a dangerous animal to be exterminated or exploited. Sharks have evolved over millions of years to be a perfect piece of the perfect puzzles that ecosystems are. As the most intelligent animal on earth, we should understand that our survival depends on the well being of our planet and all living organisms, including sharks.

We share our planet with many species of animals and plants and we should strive to respect their diversity and the environment in which they live. We need to protect wildlife, so that its richness can be enjoyed by generations to come.

GLOSSARY

ADELPHOPHAGY

THE PRACTICE OF SOME SHARK EMBRYOS FEEDING ON EACH OTHER DURING THE GESTATION PERIOD. THIS IS COMMON IN SHARKS BORN THROUGH APLACENTAL VIVIPARITY.

AGNATHA

FISH WITHOUT A JAW.

AMPHIBIAN

A COLD-BLOODED ANIMAL THAT CAN LIVE BOTH ON LAND AND IN THE WATER. AMPHIBIANS WERE THE FIRST VERTEBRATES TO WALK ON LAND, OVER 300 MILLION YEARS AGO. THEY DESCENDED FROM CERTAIN FISH CALLED LUNGFISH.

AMPULLAE OF LORENZINI

ORGANS LOCATED ON THE SNOUT OF SHARKS THAT SENSE THE ELECTRIC FIELD EMANATED BY LIVING ORGANISMS.

ANAL FINS

THE LAST SET OF FINS UNDERNEATH THE SHARK, CLOSER TO THE TAIL.

APLACENTAL VIVIPARITY

SEE *OVOVIVIPARITY*.

ARISTOTLE

(384 BC-322), AN ANCIENT GREEK PHILOSOPHER. HE STUDIED UNDER PLATO AND BECAME ALEXANDER THE GREAT'S TEACHER. ARISTOTLE WROTE BOOKS ABOUT EVERY SUBJECT, FROM NATURAL HISTORY TO GOVERNMENT AND METAPHYSICS.

BARBELS

TACTILE ORGANS, RESEMBLING A MUSTACHE, ATTACHED TO THE SNOUT OF CERTAIN SHARKS.

BASIHYAL

THE TONGUE OF SHARKS AND BONY FISH.

BATOIDS

A GROUP OF FISH WHICH INCLUDES RAYS, SKATES, GUITAR FISH, AND CHIMAERAS. THESE FISH HAVE A CARTILAGINOUS SKELETON, BUT THEY ARE NOT SHARKS.

BIOLUMINESCENCE

THE ABILITY OF SOME FISH AND SHARKS TO EMIT LIGHT.

BOROSO

IN SPAIN, IT'S THE LEATHER MADE FROM THE KITEFIN SHARK.

BOTTOM-DWELLING FISH

A FISH THAT LIVES NEAR THE BOTTOM OF A BODY OF WATER.

BRACKISH WATER

A COMBINATION OF SEA AND FRESH WATERS THAT OCCURS IN THE OCEANS NEAR RIVER ESTUARIES. IN BRACKISH WATERS THE SALINITY IS LOWER THAN ELSEWHERE IN THE OCEAN.

BRIGHT CARPET

SEE *TAPETUM LUCIDUM*.

BUOYANCY

THE ABILITY TO REMAIN AFLOAT IN A LIQUID.

CAPILLARY

A VERY SMALL BLOOD VESSEL.

CARTILAGE

THE HARD TISSUE OF WHICH SHARKS' SKELETONS ARE MADE OF.

CAUDAL FIN

THE TAIL FIN OF A SHARK.

CEPHALITIC FINS

FINS ATTACHED TO THE HEAD.

CEPHALOFOIL

THE SCIENTIFIC NAME OF THE HAMMERHEAD SHARK'S "HAMMER."

CHONDRICHTHYES

A GROUP OF FISH WITH THE SKELETON MADE OF CARTILAGE. THEY INCLUDE SHARKS, RAYS, SKATES, AND CHIMAERAS.

CLADOSELACHE

AN ANCIENT SHARK THAT LIVED DURING THE SILURIAN PERIOD, 400 MILLION YEARS AGO.

CLASPER

THE REPRODUCTIVE ORGAN OF A MALE SHARK.

DERMAL DENTICLES

SEE, *SKIN DENTICLES*.

DORSAL FIN

THE FIRST AND BIGGEST FIN ON THE BACK OF A SHARK.

ECOSYSTEM

THE COMPLEX RELATIONSHIP BETWEEN AN ENVIRONMENT AND THE ORGANISMS THAT LIVE IN IT.

ELECTROGENESIS

THE ABILITY OF CERTAIN RAYS TO GENERATE ELECTRICITY.

ELECTRORECEPTION

THE ABILITY TO SENSE THE ELECTRIC FIELD EMANATED BY A LIVING ORGANISM.

EMBRYO

A SHARK PUP BEFORE ITS BIRTH.

FOSSIL

SEE *FOSSILIZATION*.

FOSSILIZATION

A VERY SLOW PROCESS DURING WHICH THE BONES OF DEAD ANIMALS ARE GRADUALLY REPLACED BY MINERALS.

FRESHWATER FISH

FISH THAT LIVE IN WATER THAT IS NOT SALTY, LIKE LAKES AND RIVERS.

FUNGUS

ONE OF THE FIRST ORGANISMS TO GROW ON LAND, OVER 500 MILLION YEARS AGO. FUNGI ARE RELATED TO MUSHROOMS AND MOLDS.

HAKALL

AN INUIT DISH MADE WITH THE MEAT OF THE GREENLAND SLEEPER SHARK.

HETEROCERCAL TAIL

THE CAUDAL FIN IN WHICH THE UPPER AND LOWER LOBES ARE OF A DIFFERENT SIZE.

HOMINIDS

ANCESTORS OF THE HUMAN SPECIES. THEY FIRST APPEARED ABOUT TWO MILLION YEARS AGO.

HOMOCERCAL TAIL

THE CAUDAL FIN IN WHICH THE UPPER AND LOWER LOBES ARE OF THE SAME SIZE.

HYBODUS

AN ANCIENT SHARK THAT LIVED DURING THE JURASSIC PERIOD, 200 MILLION YEARS AGO.

LATERAL LINE

A BAND OF TINY PORES, CALLED NEUROMASTS, LOCATED ALONG THE SIDES OF FISH AND SHARKS. NEUROMASTS SENSE THE VIBRATIONS OF THE WATER.

LICHEN

ONE OF THE FIRST PLANTS TO GROW ON LAND, OVER 500 MILLION YEARS AGO. LICHENS ARE ORGANISMS IN WHICH FUNGI AND ALGAE LIVE SYMBIOTICALLY.

MACULA NEGLECTA

THE INTERNAL HEARING ORGAN OF A SHARK.

MAMMALS

WARM-BLOODED ANIMALS, INCLUDING HUMANS, THAT HAVE THEIR SKIN COVERED WITH HAIR. MAMMALS HAVE MAMMARY GLANDS THAT PRODUCE MILK FOR THEIR YOUNG.

MEGALODON

AN ANCIENT SHARK THAT LIVED DURING THE TERTIARY PERIOD, 20 MILLION YEARS AGO, AND BECAME EXTINCT 1.2 MILLION YEARS AGO.

MERMAID'S PURSE

THE EGGS OF CERTAIN SHARKS AND RAYS THAT ARE IN THE SHAPE OF A PURSE.

MIGRATOR

AN ANIMAL THAT SEASONALLY MOVES FROM ONE PLACE TO ANOTHER.

NASAL BARBELS

BARBELS ATTACHED TO THE NOSE OF CERTAIN SHARKS. SEE *BARBELS*.

NATURAL PHILOSOPHER

A PERSON WHO STUDIED NATURE BEFORE THE BEGINNING OF MODERN SCIENCE.

NEOPRENE

A SYNTHETIC AND WATER-RESISTANT RUBBER.

NEUROMASTS

SEE, *LATERAL LINE*.

NICTITATING MEMBRANES

THE EYELIDS OF SHARKS.

OLFACTORY LAMELLAE

ORGANS LOCATED IN THE NOSE OF SHARKS THAT SENSE SMELLS.

OOPHAGY

THE PRACTICE OF SOME SHARK EMBRYOS OF FEEDING ON THE UNHATCHED EGGS PRESENT IN THEIR MOTHER'S UTERUS DURING THE GESTATION PERIOD. THIS IS COMMON IN SHARKS BORN THROUGH APLACENTAL VIVIPARITY.

OSTEICHTHYES

A GROUP OF FISH WITH THE SKELETON MADE OF BONE.

OVIPAROUS

A WAY OF REPRODUCTION IN WHICH THE FEMALE DEPOSITS EGGS. THE EGGS HATCH OUTSIDE THE FEMALE'S BODY.

OVOVIVIPAROUS

A WAY OF REPRODUCTION IN WHICH THE EGGS HATCH INSIDE THE FEMALE'S BODY, THE EMBRYOS ARE NOT CONNECTED TO THEIR MOTHER THROUGH A PLACENTA, AND THE MOTHER GIVES BIRTH TO LIVE YOUNG.

PARASITE

AN ORGANISM THAT EXPLOITS ITS HOST. PARASITES DON'T CONTRIBUTE TO THE SURVIVAL OF THEIR HOST. THEY CAUSE HARM, AND SOMETIMES DEATH. PARASITES CAN'T SURVIVE WITHOUT A HOST.

PECTORAL FINS

THE FIRST AND BIGGEST FINS UNDERNEATH THE SHARK.

PELVIC FIN

THE SECOND SET OF FINS UNDERNEATH THE SHARK, BETWEEN THE PECTORAL AND THE ANAL FINS.

PLACENTA

A TEMPORARY ORGAN THAT CONNECTS AN EMBRYO TO ITS MOTHER DURING THE GESTATION PERIOD AND IS DISCARDED AT BIRTH. THE PLACENTA NOURISHES THE EMBRYO AND PASSES OUT ITS WASTE.

PLINY THE ELDER

GAIUS PLINIUS SECUNDUS (23-79), AN ANCIENT ROMAN NATURAL PHILOSOPHER. HE WROTE AN ENCYCLOPEDIA CALLED *NATURAL HISTORY*.

PUP

A NEWBORN SHARK.

RAM-VENTILATION

A WAY OF BREATHING WHERE SOME SHARKS HAVE TO CONTINUOUSLY SWIM IN ORDER TO LET WATER THROUGH THEIR GILLS. THESE SHARKS AREN'T ABLE TO SUCK WATER IN THEIR MOUTH.

REPTILE

AN ANIMAL WITH SCALY SKIN THAT REPRODUCES BY LAYING EGGS.

RETIA MIRABILIA

(WONDERFUL NETS) A NETWORK OF CAPILLARIES RUNNING THROUGH THE VITAL ORGANS AND MUSCLES OF MANY FISH AND MARINE MAMMALS. THE RETIA MIRABILIA RECYCLES BODY HEAT TO MAINTAIN THE BODY TEMPERATURE HIGHER THAN THE ENVIRONMENT.

SCHOOL

A GROUP OF FISH SWIMMING TOGETHER.

SERRATED TEETH

TEETH WITH JAGGED EDGES LIKE A STEAK KNIFE.

SHAGREEN

THE SKIN OF CERTAIN SHARKS AND RAYS USED BY CABINETMAKERS TO POLISH WOOD.

SHELLFISH

A MARINE INVERTEBRATE, LIKE MOLLUSKS AND CRUSTACEANS, THAT LIVES INSIDE A SHELL.

SKIN DENTICLES

SPECIALIZED SCALES THAT MAKE UP THE SKIN OF A SHARK.

SPIRACLES

OPENINGS POSITIONED NEAR THE EYES OF A SHARK. SPIRACLES AID THE SHARK IN THE BREATHING PROCESS BY LETTING WATER IN.

STETHACANTHUS

AN ANCIENT SHARK THAT LIVED DURING THE DEVONIAN PERIOD, 400 MILLION YEARS AGO.

TAGGING

A WAY TO STUDY SHARKS BY ATTACHING A TAG TO ONE. THE TAG SENDS INFORMATION ABOUT WHERE THE SHARK GOES.

TAPETUM LUCIDUM

(BRIGHT CARPET) A LAYER OF TISSUE IN THE EYES OF CERTAIN MAMMALS AND SHARKS THAT CAUSES THE EYES TO GLOW IN THE DARK. THE TAPETUM LUCIDUM REFLECTS THE INCOMING LIGHT BACK INTO THE EYES, INCREASING THE ABILITY TO SEE IN DIM LIGHT.

TENDRIL

THE STRINGS OR HOOKS OF SHARK EGGS.

THEOCODONT

ANCIENT REPTILE ANCESTORS OF THE DINOSAURS. THEY LIVED ON EARTH OVER 250 MILLION YEARS AGO.

UMBILICAL CORD

A TUBE THAT CONNECTS AN EMBRYO TO ITS MOTHER'S PLACENTA.

UNPROVOKED SHARK ATTACK

A SHARK ATTACK THAT WASN'T DIRECTLY PROVOKED BY A DIVER.

UTERINE MILK

A WHITE SUBSTANCE SECRETED BY THE MOTHER TO NOURISH THE EMBRYOS. THIS IS COMMON IN SHARKS BORN THROUGH APLACENTAL VIVIPARITY.

UTERUS

(WOMB) THE REPRODUCTIVE ORGAN IN WHICH EMBRYOS DEVELOP DURING THE GESTATION PERIOD.

VERTICAL MIGRATOR

SHARKS THAT ROUTINELY MOVE UP AND DOWN THE WATER COLUMN.

VIVIPAROUS

A WAY OF REPRODUCTION IN WHICH THE FEMALE GIVES BIRTH TO LIVE YOUNG.

WONDERFUL NETS

SEE *RETIA MIRABILIA*

XENACANTHUS

AN ANCIENT SHARK THAT LIVED DURING THE CARBONIFEROUS PERIOD, 300 MILLION YEARS AGO.

ZOOPLANKTON

THE COLLECTIVE NAME OF MICROSCOPIC AQUATIC ORGANISMS, SUCH AS CRUSTACEANS, LARVAE, AND WORMS.